Other Publications:

HOME REPAIR
AND IMPROVEMENT

HOME SECURITY

BY THE EDITORS OF
TIME-LIFE BOOKS

TIME-LIFE BOOKS
ALEXANDRIA, VIRGINIA

Time-Life Books Inc.
is a wholly owned subsidiary of
TIME INCORPORATED

Founder Henry R. Luce 1898-1967

Editor-in-Chief Hedley Donovan
Chairman of the Board Andrew Heiskell
President James R. Shepley
Vice Chairmen Roy E. Larsen, Arthur Temple
Corporate Editors Ralph Graves, Henry Anatole Grunwald

TIME-LIFE BOOKS INC.

Managing Editor Jerry Korn
Executive Editor David Maness
Assistant Managing Editors Dale M. Brown (planning), George Constable,
Jim Hicks (acting), Martin Mann, John Paul Porter
Art Director Tom Suzuki
Chief of Research David L. Harrison
Director of Photography Robert G. Mason
Senior Text Editor Diana Hirsh
Assistant Art Director Arnold C. Holeywell
Assistant Chief of Research Carolyn L. Sackett
Assistant Director of Photography Dolores A. Littles

Chairman Joan D. Manley
President John D. McSweeney
Executive Vice Presidents Carl G. Jaeger, John Steven Maxwell, David J. Walsh
Vice Presidents Peter G. Barnes (comptroller), Nicholas Benton
(public relations), John L. Canova (sales),
Nicholas J. C. Ingleton (Asia), James L. Mercer
(Europe/South Pacific), Herbert Sorkin (production),
Paul R. Stewart (promotion)
Personnel Director Beatrice T. Dobie
Consumer Affairs Director Carol Flaumenhaft

HOME REPAIR AND IMPROVEMENT

Editorial Staff for Home Security

Editor William Frankel
Assistant Editor Lee Hassig
Designer Kenneth E. Hancock
Picture Editor Adrian Allen
Text Editors Russell B. Adams Jr., Richard Flanagan, Bob Menaker,
Mark M. Steele, David Thiemann
Staff Writers Lynn R. Addison, Megan Barnett, Stephen Brown,
Alan Epstein, Steven J. Forbis, Geoffrey B. Henning,
Leslie Marshall, Brooke Stoddard, William Worsley
Art Associates George Bell, Daniel J. McSweeney,
Lorraine D. Rivard, Richard Whiting
Editorial Assistant Susanne S. Trice

Editorial Production

Production Editor Douglas B. Graham
Operations Manager Gennaro C. Esposito, Gordon E. Buck (assistant)
Assistant Production Editor Feliciano Madrid
Quality Control Robert L. Young (director), James J. Cox (assistant),
Michael G. Wight (associate)
Art Coordinator Anne B. Landry
Copy Staff Susan B. Galloway (chief), Margery duMond,
Celia Beattie
Picture Department Renee DeSandies
Traffic Jeanne Potter

Correspondents: Elisabeth Kraemer (Bonn); Margot
Hapgood, Dorothy Bacon (London); Susan Jonas,
Lucy T. Voulgaris (New York); Maria Vincenza Aloisi,
Josephine du Brusle (Paris); Ann Natanson (Rome).
Valuable assistance was also provided by Carolyn T.
Chubet, Miriam Hsia (New York).

THE CONSULTANTS: Jon Payne owns a firm that
specializes in locks and safes for homes and
small businesses.

Thomas F. Smith, president of a burglar- and fire-
alarm company, is an electrical engineer and electrician in several counties and states.

Wayne Carson is a fire-prevention engineer whose
firm designs fire-safety systems.

Charles Hughes, who has served as vice-chairman of
the Washington, D.C., chapter of the American
Welding Society, is a welding instructor.

Roswell W. Ard is a consulting structural engineer
and a professional home inspector in northern Michi-
gan. He has written professional papers on wood-
frame construction techniques.

Harris Mitchell, special consultant for Canada, has
worked in the field of home repair and improvement
for more than two decades. He is editor of the maga-
zine *Canadian Homes* and author of a syndicated
newspaper column, "You Wanted to Know," as well
as a number of books on home improvement.

Library of Congress Cataloging in Publication Data
Time-Life Books.
    Home Security
    (Home repair and improvement, v. 16)
    includes index.
    1. Dwellings—Security Measures I. Title
9345.D85T55   1979   643   78-27634
ISBN 0-8094-2420-7
ISBN 0-8094-2419-3 lib. bdg.

Contents

Barriers against Break-ins

Not many years ago most Americans left their house doors unlocked. Children coming home from school expected to be able to walk into the house even if Mother had gone off shopping. Only Father owned a front-door key, and back-door locks—if used—were so rudimentary that anyone could pick one with a hairpin.

Statistics explain why that easy life style has become a nostalgic memory, and personal security has become a major concern for almost everyone. Since World War II, the burglary rate has been rising steadily in cities, suburbs and rural areas; there no longer are any "safe" towns or neighborhoods. Public concern about this trend is reflected in the money spent on defenses against criminals: In one four-year period, sales of locks rose more than 65 per cent and sales of steel grilles for doors and windows rose more than 40 per cent; in the same period, the sales of home burglar alarms more than doubled. For some, security has become an obsession. In crime-ridden areas, people install so many locks that some have been trapped and killed by fire while firemen vainly tried to break in.

Fire, in fact, is a greater danger to personal safety than burglary (Chapter 3); 780,000 home fires occur each year, killing nearly 8,000 people. Even more threatening than fire, however, are household accidents (Chapter 4), which kill 19,000 people and disable about 210,000 annually. A safe and secure home requires protection against all these hazards—an alarm system should warn of fire as well as burglary; a fence may be needed not so much to keep an intruder out as to keep a toddler or a pet in.

But burglary remains a principal concern, largely because most homes, even if newly built, are poorly equipped to bar intrusion. Simple improvements—a fence that is difficult to scale (left and pages 8-13), locks that cannot be jimmied or picked (pages 20-39), a few strategically placed yard lights (pages 14-19)—can persuade would-be burglars to try their luck elsewhere. How elaborate you make your defenses depends on your evaluation of the risk, based on your own experience and that of friends and acquaintances. Burglary is a lesser threat in an urban or suburban neighborhood where friendly neighbors are always around to keep an eye on things than in an impersonal apartment complex or a remote farmhouse.

Every measure you take involves compromises, even when you follow professional advice. Policemen often recommend barred windows and doors, yet firemen prefer open entryways for quick rescues; police object to the fences homeowners like because such barriers impede pursuit of a fleeing criminal. The common-sense choices described on the following pages can give your family the reasonable protection it needs, simply and economically.

A Chain Link Fence at the Property Line

Any fence defining your property line is a psychological barrier to illegal entry, but a high chain link fence is a formidable physical obstacle as well. Difficult to scale, it slows or prevents entry, but more important to a potential burglar, it severely hampers exit, making removal of valuables awkward even for an athletic criminal and exposing him to view.

Chain link is not only effective; it is also inexpensive and easily installed. Two workers can erect 300 to 500 feet of fencing, complete with gates, in a weekend. The lightweight wire mesh requires support posts spaced no more than 10 feet apart. They must be set in concrete only in rocky or very sandy soil; elsewhere metal anchors, which need only shallow

holes, simplify the job, eliminating the mess and labor of concrete and the two-day delay required for it to harden.

The least expensive and most common type of chain link fencing, galvanized to prevent rust, weathers to a dull gray. At additional cost, you can buy mesh and posts with a colored vinyl coating over the galvanized steel; dark green is popular because it blends with shrubbery to make fencing virtually invisible.

Where you can place a fence and how high it can be are generally regulated by laws and building codes. Many localities prohibit a fence more than 4 feet high in a front yard or 6 feet in a backyard. Regardless of law, it is usually wise to set a fence at least a foot or so inside your

property line. An error that causes the fence to infringe on a neighbor's property is embarrassing and could prove costly.

Before ordering materials, draw a rough map of fence lines to scale. Mark locations for line posts and for the thicker terminal posts needed at ends, gates and corners and at the tops and bottoms of slopes of more than 1 foot in 4. Using the map, a fence distributor can supply wire mesh, posts and hardware for the job. Many distributors also rent special tools, such as fence pliers, cutters for mesh, a stretcher bar *(page 12, Step 2)* and a cable jack, or "comealong," to make it taut, and a post driver—a heavy, capped pipe slipped over a post to hammer it into the ground.

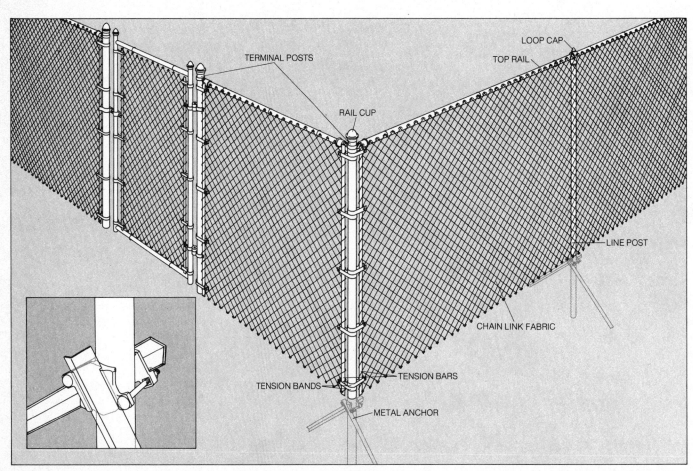

Anatomy of a chain link fence. Every component of this fence—the posts, the wire-mesh fabric and the hardware—is prefabricated. Heavy-duty terminal posts at corners, ends and gateways and the lighter line posts between

terminals, set 24 to 30 inches into the ground and secured with metal anchors *(inset)*, hold the wire mesh. A top rail, running through looped caps on the line posts and secured to the terminal posts with fittings called rail cups, provides

lateral support. Metal tension bars, slipped through links of mesh and clamped to terminal posts with circular clips called tension bands, tighten the mesh during installation. Tie wires attach mesh to line posts and top rails.

Setting Up the Posts

1 Digging the postholes. Drive stakes to mark the locations of corner, gate and terminal posts, and have a helper measure and mark the height of the fence down from the tops of the terminal posts. String a line between the corner and end stakes and mark the line in equal segments of 10 feet or less. Remove the stakes and, using a posthole digger or a shovel, dig any necessary holes for line and terminal posts. For concrete footings make holes 12 inches deep by 12 inches wide. Some metal anchors require no holes; others are started in holes 4 inches deep by 10 inches wide.

In locations where the property slopes more than 1 in 4 feet between gates or corners, dig the holes for extra terminal posts at the top and bottom of each slope.

2 Driving the posts. Center the terminal posts in their holes and, while a helper with a torpedo level holds the posts plumb, drive them down with a post driver until the mark on each post is even with the ground. String a line 2 inches below the tops of the terminal posts and drive the line posts until their tops are level with the line.

If you cannot rent a post driver similar to the one illustrated, hold a block of wood over the top of the post as a protective buffer, and drive the post with a sledge hammer.

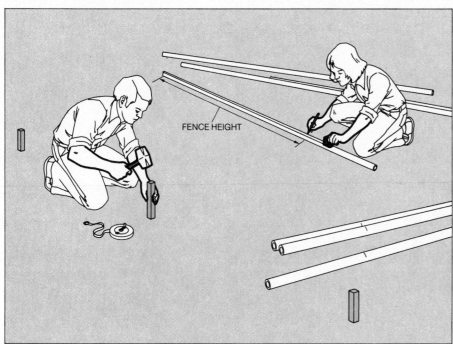

FENCE HEIGHT

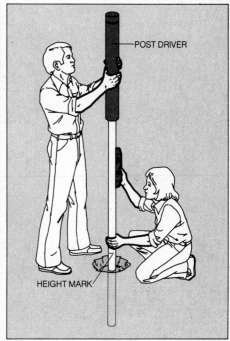

POST DRIVER

HEIGHT MARK

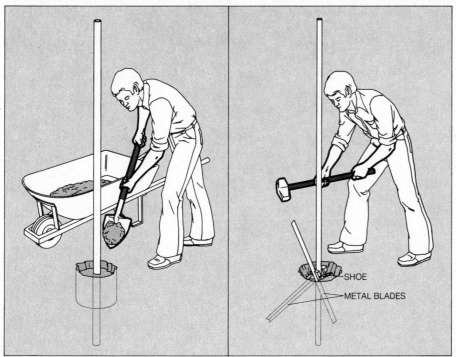

SHOE

METAL BLADES

3 Anchoring the posts. To anchor a post with concrete *(far left)*, fill the posthole with a thick mix of 1 part cement, 3 parts sand, 5 parts gravel and from ¾ to 1 part water—or, if you prefer, use premixed concrete and water. Overfill the hole slightly and use a trowel to bevel the concrete down from the post so that rain will run off. Let the concrete set for 48 hours.

To anchor a post with a metal anchor *(near left)*, bolt the anchor shoe loosely to the post, insert the metal blades in the shoe slots and strike the blades with a 12-pound sledge to drive them into the ground at right angles to the fence line. Tighten the bolts on the shoe. If you are using metal anchors in sandy soil, attach a second shoe and drive another set of blades at right angles to the first.

Installing the Top Rails

1 **Supports for the rail.** Bolt a pair of rail bands and cups at right angles, 2 inches below the top of a corner post; to set the centers of both cups at the same level, reverse the offsets on the cups. Repeat the procedure at an adjacent terminal post. Slip loop caps over the intervening line posts, and slide a 20-foot section of top rail through the caps of two adjacent line posts and into a rail cup. Insert additional sections, sliding the crimped end of each section into the end of the preceding one (*inset*) until a section extends beyond the far terminal post.

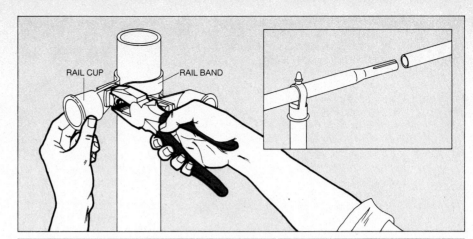

RAIL CUP · RAIL BAND

2 **Cutting the top rail to fit.** At the far terminal, mark the loose end of the rail ⅛ inch from the inner end of the cup, and hacksaw the rail at the mark; then turn the cup upward, place the cut end of the rail against the lower lip of the cup (*inset*) and push both the rail and the cup downward until they lock together.

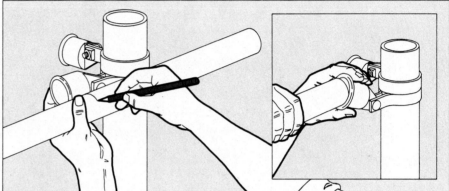

Hanging the Chain Link Fabric

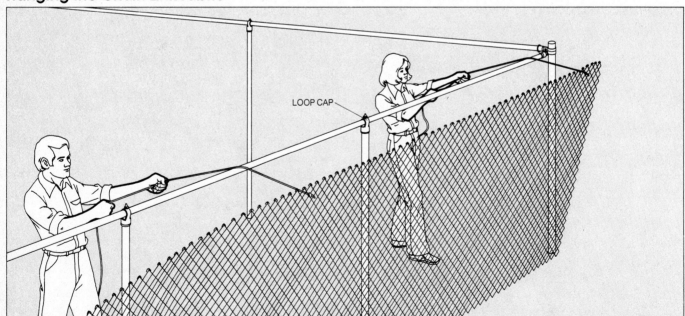

LOOP CAP

1 **Raising the fabric into place.** Set a roll of chain link fabric near a terminal post—an uphill one if the land slopes—and unroll the fabric on the ground along the outside of the post-and-rail framework; then tie ropes to the upper edge of the fabric at the end of the roll and at a point 15 feet from the end, run the two ropes over the top rail, and pull the fabric up against the line posts and the top rail. Secure the fabric temporarily to the top rail with tie wires at intervals of 5 feet. Continue raising the fabric by the same method until you reach the far terminal post. (If you use up the roll between terminal posts, add a new one as indicated opposite, bottom). With a helper, pull the fabric taut to the far terminal post. Make the top of the chain link even with the top rail—if it is higher, dig a trench below the wire and push the top edge down.

2 **Fitting the fabric to the terminal post.** Weave
a tension bar down through the row of diamonds
nearest the terminal post used as a starting
point, slip tension bands around the terminal post
at 1½-foot intervals, with the flat side of each
band on the outside face of the fence; then pull
the tension bar between the jaws of the bands,
and install bolts and nuts to clamp the jaws shut.

If you are installing the fence on a slope, have a
helper stretch the fabric past the terminal
post, and weave the tension bar parallel to the
plumb terminal post *(inset);* you will have
to skip some links of the fabric to keep the bar
plumb. Attach the bar to the post with tension
bands, cut off the excess fabric and bend the
loose fabric strands around the bar.

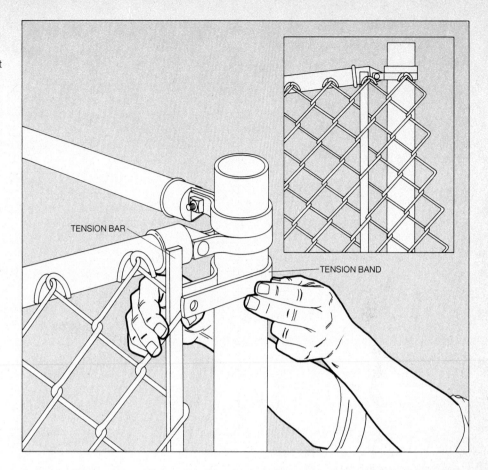

TENSION BAR

TENSION BAND

How to Make a Splice

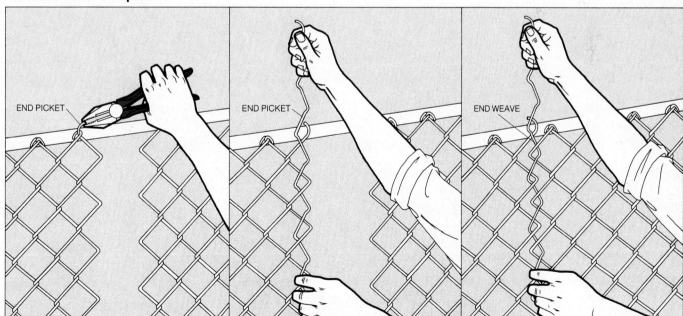

END PICKET

END PICKET

END WEAVE

Weaving the wire. When you come to the
end of the first roll, hoist alongside it one end of a
fresh roll, following the procedure of Step 1,
and, using fence pliers, loosen the top and bottom
wires of the end strand, or picket *(left).* Pull

the picket from the wire weave by screwing it
corkscrew-fashion out of the mesh *(center).*
Pull the two rolls of fabric together, and weave the
picket strand back down through the end
weaves of the first roll *(right).*

Tightening the Fabric

1 **Attaching the cable jack.** About 4 or 5 feet from the far terminal post, have a helper weave a tension bar through the fabric. Hook the cable of a cable jack around the post, and hook the other end to a stretcher bar—a flat 3-foot bar with a hook at the center of one edge and three hooks on the other. Slip the hooks of the stretcher bar over the tension bar.

On a fence that is more than 4 feet high, use two cable jacks and two stretcher bars, located on the top and bottom halves of the fence; on a lower fence, use a single stretcher-bar assembly at the middle of the fence.

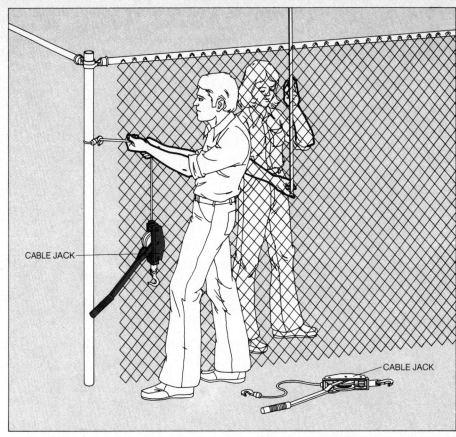

CABLE JACK

CABLE JACK

2 **Stretching the fabric.** While a helper moves along the fence, lifting the fabric so it clears the ground, work the handles of the cable jacks to pull the fabric taut. Stretch the fabric until the rows of its diamond weave are quite straight.

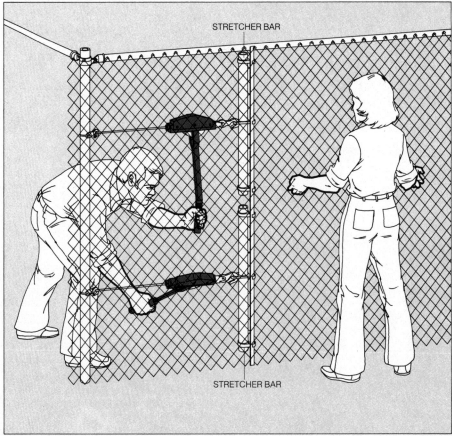

STRETCHER BAR

STRETCHER BAR

3 **Fastening fabric to the far terminal.** Weave a second tension bar into the fabric 4 inches from the terminal post and tighten the jacks until the bar is next to the post; then slip tension bands around the post and bolt the bar and bands together *(page 11, Step 2)*. On land that slopes, align the second tension bar so that it is parallel with the terminal post. Cut off excess chain link with fence pliers, release the jacks and remove the stretcher bars and the first tension bar. (For clarity, the excess chain link is shown stretched out in the picture at right.)

4 **Securing the fabric to the line posts.** Working inside the fence at each of the line posts, slip the pigtail of a tie wire around a strand of chain link 8 inches below the top rail, turn the wire around the post and twist it around a link of chain. Install additional tie wires down the posts at intervals of 12 to 18 inches.

Make a final adjustment of the fabric to set it even with the top rail and, at 2-foot intervals, wrap a tie wire around the rail and through the chain link, twisting the ends together underneath the top rail *(inset)*.

Set terminal post caps over the terminal posts and lightly tap them into place with a hammer.

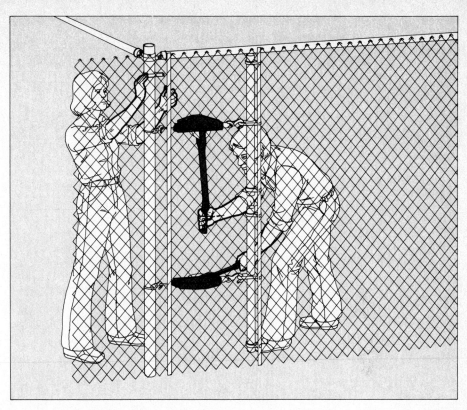

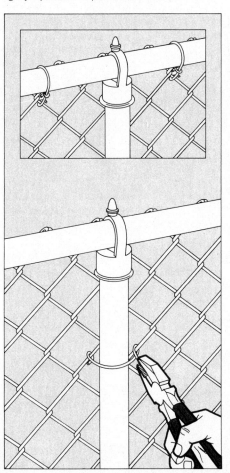

Ready-made Gates for Walks and Driveways

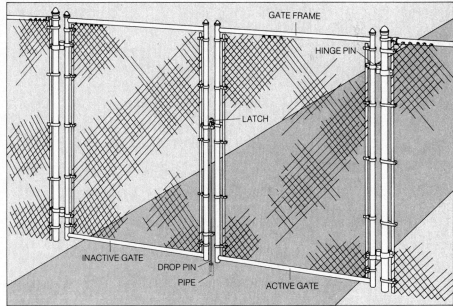

GATE FRAME

HINGE PIN

LATCH

INACTIVE GATE

DROP PIN

PIPE

ACTIVE GATE

Installing gates. When the fence is complete, bolt the solid gate hinges loosely to one of the gateposts, with the top hinge pin pointing down and the bottom pin pointing up. Bolt the hollow hinges loosely to the gate frame, place the gate next to the post and slide the hollow hinges over the hinge pins. Adjust the hinges until the top of the gate frame is even with the top rail, then tighten all the bolts securely.

On a double gate, use the same techniques to install the second gate and to even the top gate rails, then bolt the latch to the active gate, close the gates and let the latch fall. Loosen the drop pin on the inactive gate and let it drop to the ground. Mark its location. In a concrete or asphalt walk or driveway, use a carbide bit to drill a hole for the pin; in dirt or gravel, drive a pipe ½ inch wider than the pin to act as a stop.

Low-Cost Floodlights for the House and Grounds

Night prowlers tend to pass by a lighted yard and house rather than risk being noticed by neighbors and passersby. The light does not have to be bright—an artificial equivalent of bright moonlight will do. And you can provide the light in a variety of ways.

The ideal security lights are powerful mercury-vapor lamps mounted on tall trees or poles about 50 feet from the house, to bathe the house and yard with even, unobtrusive light—but a system of this kind is so difficult to set up and so expensive that it is practical only in special cases. Most people settle for a less effective scheme, relying on incandescent floodlights mounted on the house itself, but these lights generally cast black shadows that conceal prowlers. In an effective compromise between the two methods, you can light whole sides of your house with a single mercury-vapor lamp mounted in a special utility fixture *(pages 16-17)* or in a rewired lamppost fixture *(pages 18-19)*, and use incandescent floodlights to fill in any dark spots created by trees or terrain. If you equip each fixture with an electric-eye switch, your system will turn itself on and off automatically as necessary.

The incandescent floodlights cost less to buy than mercury-vapor bulbs and have the advantage of being aimable, so that you can illuminate vulnerable doors and windows without lighting the entire yard. Mercury-vapor bulbs are more economical and convenient in the long run: they emit twice as much light for each watt of electricity and last up to 10 times as long as incandescents.

Mercury-vapor lamps do have two disadvantages that you should consider in designing a lighting system. Standard "clear" mercury-vapor bulbs emit a harsh, bluish light better suited to an industrial district than to a residential neighborhood (you can reduce the glare by using slightly more expensive "de luxe white" bulbs, which give a softer, more balanced light). And high-wattage fixtures may simply be too powerful for some situations. The 175-watt utility fixture shown opposite, for example, emits as much light as a city street lamp; it should not be mounted directly above one of your windows or within 50 feet of a neighbor's windows.

Wall-mounted mercury-vapor fixtures, available through electrical suppliers and large mail-order houses, come complete with an electrical ballast to regulate the current, an electric-eye switch to turn the bulb on at dusk and off at dawn, and a special bulb. (Fixtures that come with "self-ballasted" bulbs are not recommended; they cost as much as a standard mercury-vapor fixture but use as much electricity as an incandescent lamp.)

To adapt an ordinary lamppost fixture for a mercury-vapor bulb, buy separate components at an electrical-supply store and connect them yourself. You will need a bulb that fits inside the hood of the fixture, a ballast that matches the wattage of the bulb and fits inside the pole, and an electric-eye switch housed in a short length of lamppost tubing.

Before putting in any of these lamps, consider the existing light sources around your house—street lights, lampposts already standing in your yard and floodlights already mounted on the house.

To find out where you need additional illumination, walk around the house at a distance of about 40 feet on a moonless night and have a helper in dark clothes stand next to each ground-floor door and window; at the same time, check any second-story windows that might be accessible—from a garage or porch roof, for example, or an overhanging tree. Wherever the helper is hidden by trees and shrubbery you should prune to improve visibility; wherever he blends into the shadows you should augment the existing light. Aim these lights downward—lights aimed out into the yard create deep shadows next to the house that could hide a prowler, and their glare may blind anyone who might otherwise notice the intruder.

The wiring for a security-lighting system is simplest if you can tap power from an electrical junction or outlet box in the basement or attic, or from an outlet alongside each fixture. Make sure the circuit is 120 volts, not one of the 240-volt circuits that feed dryers, ranges and some air conditioners.

Nearly any outlet that has two cables entering it contains a power source—a hot supply wire uninterrupted by a switch. However, a junction box may contain switch-controlled wires unsuitable for tapping. To be sure there is a hot supply wire, cut all power at the service panel and unscrew the wire cap from a connection that has at least one black wire. Test to be sure power is off, holding one probe of a voltage tester against the bare wires and one against a bare copper ground wire; the tester light should not glow. Hold the probes in the same position while a helper restores power; if the wire is hot the light will glow.

Take common-sense precautions when you do the wiring. Never work on a live circuit; when working at a junction box, switch off all power to the house, because wires from more than one circuit may run through the box. And before you begin to work, check all wires with the voltage tester to make sure power is off. In some localities an electrical permit may be required.

A sample lighting system. Few houses have exactly the same situation and lighting requirements as the example below, but the principles illustrated here can be applied to almost any house. The mercury-vapor lamppost fixture in front of this house illuminates the front door, the windows on both sides of the door and most of the front yard. The shadow cast over the garage door and driveway by the retaining wall is eliminated by an incandescent flood light that is aimed down at the door. Both the right side and the back of the house are illuminated by a single bright mercury-vapor utility fixture. A street light illuminates the entire left side of the house; no new fixtures are needed there.

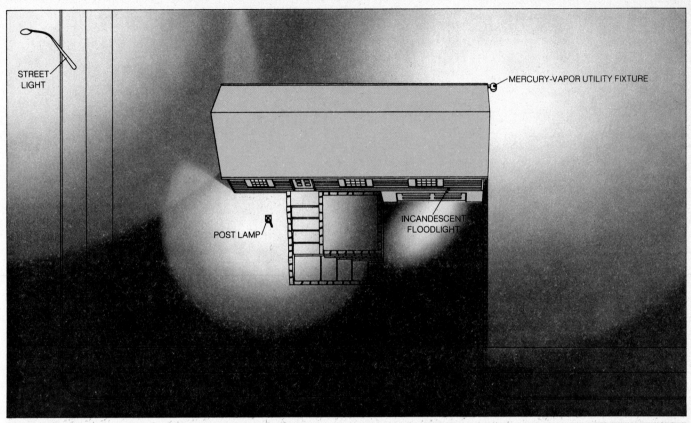

STREET LIGHT

MERCURY-VAPOR UTILITY FIXTURE

POST LAMP

INCANDESCENT FLOODLIGHT

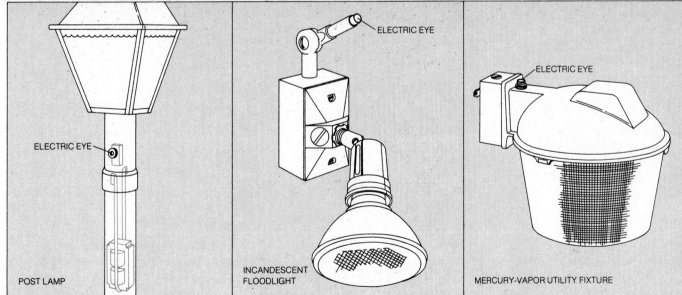

POST LAMP

ELECTRIC EYE

ELECTRIC EYE

INCANDESCENT FLOODLIGHT

ELECTRIC EYE

MERCURY-VAPOR UTILITY FIXTURE

Three types of security lamps. The lamppost fixture at left has been adapted for mercury-vapor security lighting with two additions: an electrical ballast hanging inside the post, and a section of tubing that houses an electric-eye switch. The lamp illuminates a circle about 30 feet in diameter. The incandescent spotlight at center is controlled by a wand-type electric-eye switch; the light is aimed by pivoting the lamp-holder arm and casts a narrow cone of light with a base diameter roughly equal to the height of the fixture above the ground. The 175-watt mercury-vapor utility fixture at right has a built-in ballast and electric eye; when mounted high above the ground, it lights a circle about 80 feet wide.

Running a Cable for an Outside Light

Tapping power. With power shut off, connect the wires of a new cable to a hot cable at a junction or outlet box, enlarging this box with extenders if necessary to hold the added wires. To begin this step, remove a circular knockout from the box and install a cable connector in the knockout hole; then thread a No. 14 outdoor cable into the box and tighten the connector clamp onto the cable. Using wire caps large enough to accommodate the extra wire, make the connections—black wire to black, white to white, and the bare copper ground wire to the bare or green wires. Replace the box cover.

Outside the house, drill a 1-inch hole at the planned location of the new lamp. Run the new cable through the hole and fasten the cable with cable staples every 4 feet.

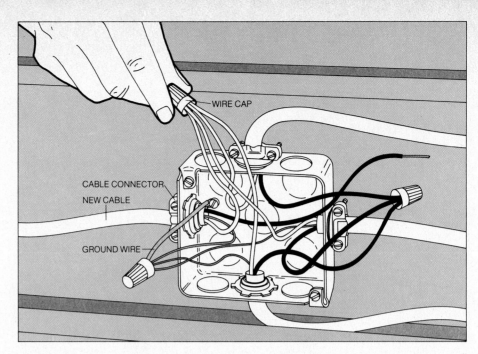

WIRE CAP

CABLE CONNECTOR

NEW CABLE

GROUND WIRE

A Mercury-vapor Utility Lamp

1 Mounting a weatherproof outlet box. Outside the house, slide the four pieces of a weatherproof cable connector (*inset*) over the end of the cable and tighten the connector, then hold the connector with pliers and screw an outdoor outlet box onto it through the threaded hole in the back of the box. Set the connector in the hole you drilled in the exterior of the house—in this example, in the fascia—and screw the box in place through the hinged mounting tabs.

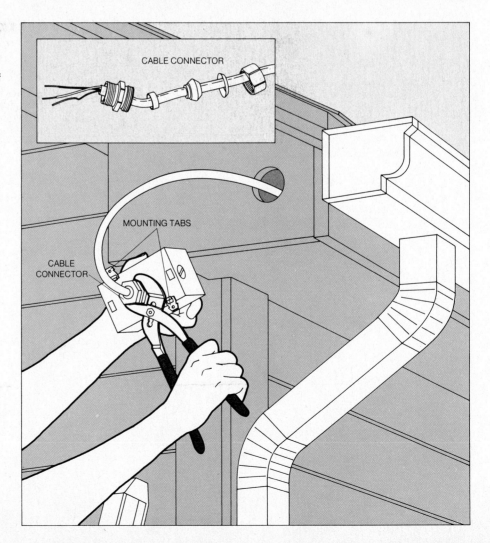

CABLE CONNECTOR

MOUNTING TABS

CABLE CONNECTOR

2 Wiring the fixture. Screw together the threaded nipple and the strap that come with the lamp fixture, and fasten the strap to tabs of the outlet box with the screws provided. Connect one grounding jumper—a 6-inch length of green insulated wire—to the green grounding screw on the back of the fixture, and another to the grounding screw of the outdoor box. As a helper holds the fixture, use wire caps to connect the jumpers to the bare wire of the cable, and make the connections between the other fixture and cable wires—white to white and black to black.

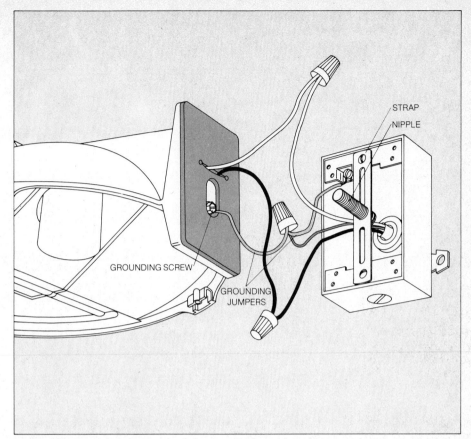

STRAP

NIPPLE

GROUNDING SCREW

GROUNDING JUMPERS

3 Mounting the fixture. Slide the metal hood of the fixture over the nipple and screw a cap nut onto the nipple until the hood gasket is tight against the outlet box. Fit the doughnut-shaped plastic lens to the fixture with the clips provided by the manufacturer, then screw the mercury-vapor bulb into its socket.

To test the lamp, restore power and cover the electric eye on top of the hood with black tape; the lamp should turn on in about one minute.

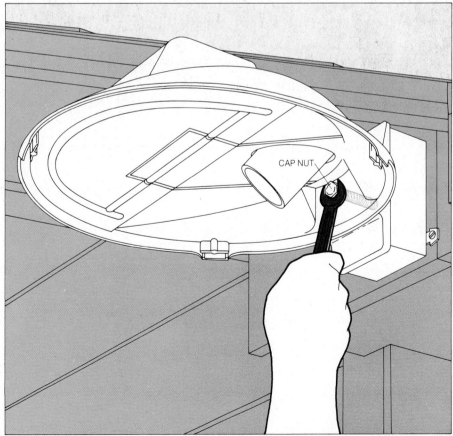

CAP NUT

Adapting a Yard Light to a Mercury-vapor Bulb

1 **Connecting the ballast and electric eye.** With power off, remove the incandescent fixture from the top of the lamppost and disconnect its wires, then have a helper hold the ballast and the electric eye while you connect their wires to the cable inside the post. Using wire caps, join the white wires of the cable and the electric eye to the ballast wire marked COMMON, the black cable wire to the black wire of the electric eye, and the red wire of the electric eye to the ballast wire marked 120 VOLTS or LINE. Do not, at this point, connect the wires marked LAMP and LAMP COMMON. Extend the bare ground wire of the cable with a 1-foot length of green insulated wire.

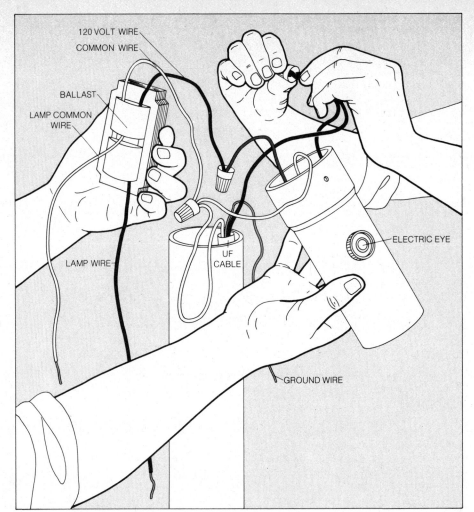

120 VOLT WIRE
COMMON WIRE
BALLAST
LAMP COMMON WIRE
LAMP WIRE
UF CABLE
ELECTRIC EYE
GROUND WIRE

2 **Mounting the ballast and eye.** Set the ballast, with the lamp and lamp common wires up, into the U-shaped strap provided by the manufacturer, lower the strap into the lamppost and hook the tabs at the ends of the strap over the outside of the post. Thread the lamp, lamp common and cable ground wires through the tubing that houses the electric eye. Fit the bottom of the tubing over the top of the lamppost and, using holes in the tubing as a template, drill holes in the post. Fasten the tubing with the self-tapping screws provided by the manufacturer.

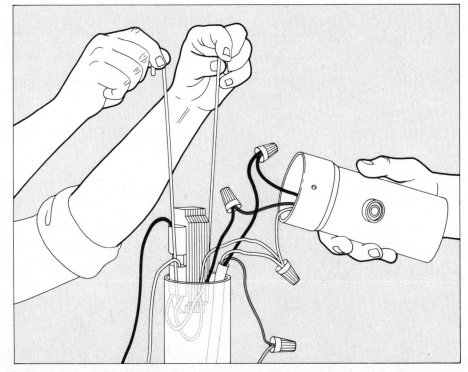

3 **Wiring the lamp fixture.** Have a helper hold the fixture while you make connections with wire caps: the lamp's green or bare ground wire to the green cable wire, the lamp's white wire to the ballast wire marked LAMP COMMON, and the lamp's black wire to the ballast wire marked LAMP. Slide the fixture over the top of the electric-eye tubing, use the holes in the bottom of the fixture as a template to drill matching holes in the tubing and screw the lamp to the tubing.

Install a mercury-vapor bulb that matches the wattage of the ballast and has a "medium base," designed to fit a standard lamp socket. Test the lamp fixture *(page 17, Step 3).*

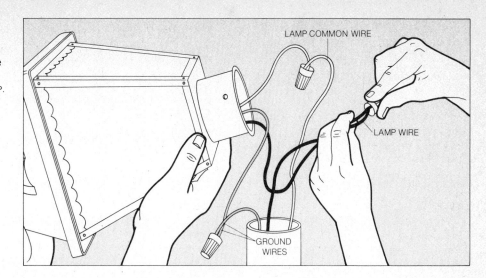

LAMP COMMON WIRE

LAMP WIRE

GROUND WIRES

Mounting an Incandescent Flood Lamp

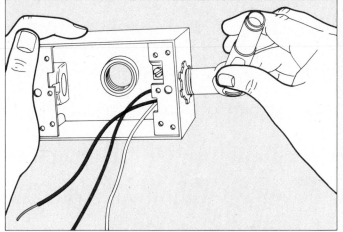

1 **Installing the box and electric eye.** Thread the wires of a wand-type electric-eye switch through the hole at one end of an outdoor outlet, screw the switch into the box and tighten the star nut. Using the techniques shown on pages 16 and 17, run cable from a junction box to the outlet box and mount the outlet box, aiming the wand of the electric eye toward the sky.

2 **Wiring the lamp holder.** Attach a weather-proof lamp holder in the threaded opening in the outlet-box cover and tighten the star nut; slide the gasket over the lamp-holder wires and connect the wires with wire caps. Connect the bare ground wire of the supply cable to the grounding screw of the outlet box, join all white wires, connect the black cable wire to the black wire from the electric eye, and connect the eye's red wire to the lamp holder's black wire.

Screw the cover plate to the outlet box, making sure that the gasket seats snugly. Install a weatherproof 75-watt incandescent floodlight, aim the lamp and test *(page 17, Step 3).*

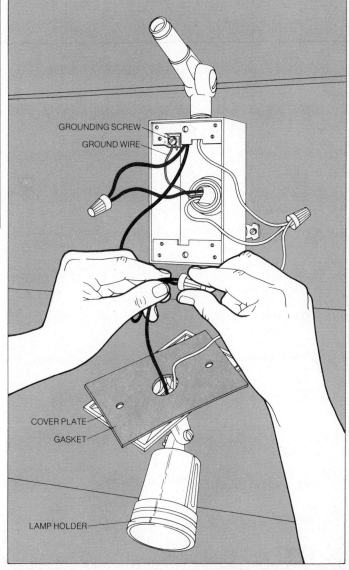

GROUNDING SCREW

GROUND WIRE

COVER PLATE

GASKET

LAMP HOLDER

Corrective Surgery for Vulnerable Doorways

Most exterior doors are strong enough to be made virtually impregnable. There are exceptions to this rule. A hollow-core flush door—occasionally used because it is inexpensive—is so flimsy that a child could kick it in. If you want a wooden door, the most secure is the type known as staved solid-core—laminated 2-by-4s covered with veneer; ordinary solid-core doors are veneer over particle board, which is not very sturdy. If you want a metal door, be sure that the steel is 16 gauge or thicker.

For greatest security, exterior doors should be windowless, and mail slots or other openings should be placed as far from the latch as possible. To see who is outside, install a viewer *(below)*; models with a 180° field of view make it impossible for anyone to duck out of sight.

Unfortunately, even the sturdiest doors are often installed in ways that make a break-in easy. The principal weakness is in the fasteners. Hinges, locks, even special security chains may be screwed on so inadequately that a paper boy's innocent push can pop the entire mechanism free. Hinge screws, for example, may be short, penetrating no deeper than the door

jamb. Such screws are adequate in a steel jamb, but in a wooden one they offer little resistance to a pry bar; replace them with 3-inch No. 10 wood screws that extend into the stud behind the jamb.

A long screw is next to useless, however, unless you drive it into a predrilled hole of exactly the right size—or sizes. The hole for a sheet-metal screw is the same width for its entire length; a hole for a wood screw has two widths—narrow for the threads and wider for the shank—and must be drilled in two stages *(opposite, top)*.

Because wood is easy to cut, wooden doors and jambs need additional reinforcement. Steel bars driven into a solid-core, flush wooden door above and below a lock *(page 22)* make it extremely hard to saw or chop the lock out of the door. Paneled wooden doors are not easily protected against cutting, since the panels are too thin for reinforcement. In most wooden doors with a dead-bolt lock, the door strike—the receptacle for the bolt—is not much more than a hole bored into the wood; if you have such a strike, replace it with a maximum-security type *(page 22)*, which encloses the bolt

in a metal shell called a strike box.

Many wooden jambs are flexible and can be levered away from the door far enough to free the bolt or latch and open the door. A properly installed door does not have this defect: its jambs are rigid, because they are shimmed behind the hinges on one side of the door and behind the strike on the other. But not every jamb has shims where they are needed. The only way to tell is to remove the interior casing; inspect the spaces immediately outside the jambs and add plywood fillers and pairs of cedar shims as necessary *(page 24)*.

Finally, there are doors and doorways that are vulnerable because of their design. If an exterior door opens out of the house, the best lock and the sturdiest door can be defeated simply by pulling out the exposed hinge pins and taking down the door—unless the hinges are pinned in a special way *(page 25)*. Sliding glass doors are especially easy to remove if the movable panel can be lifted out of the lower track. A few screws driven into the upper track *(page 25)* removes this hazard by making it impossible to raise the panel when the door is closed.

Installing a wide-angle viewer. At the center of the door, at a height convenient to the eyes of family members, drill a hole as wide as the viewer-shank—usually ½ inch—then insert the two halves of the viewer and screw them together. Screw the sections thumb-tight if the interior section is knurled; if it is slotted, use a coin to make the viewer snug.

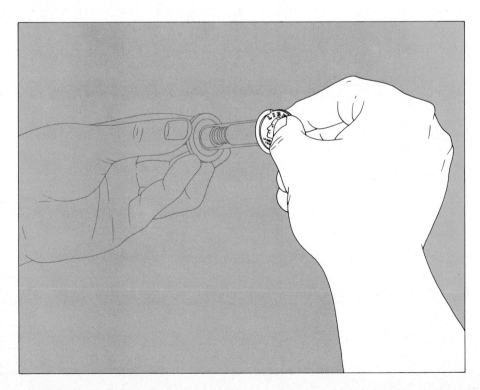

Holes to Grip Screws Tight

1 The pilot hole. With a drill bit of the size required by the screw (*chart, below*), bore a hole for the threads of the screw. Tape the bit so that this pilot hole extends 1/16 inch deeper than the combined length of the screw's threaded and shank sections. (A fully driven screw is also shown, to indicate the depth of the pilot hole.)

2 Making room for the shank. Bore into the pilot hole with a bit that matches the screw's shank-hole diameter as listed in the chart. Tape the bit so that you are able to avoid enlarging the pilot hole below the depth of the shank.

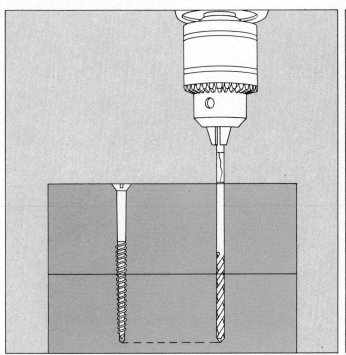

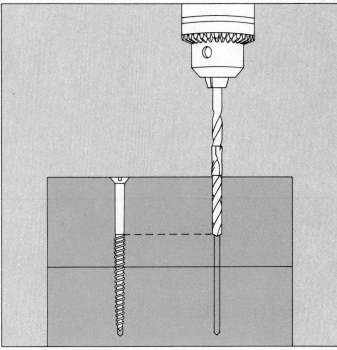

Matching Bits to Screws

Bits for pilot and shank holes. This chart specifies the sizes of bits needed to make tightly gripping pilot and shank holes for seven common gauges of wood screw. If you are using sheet-metal screws, drill the pilot hole only. If screws supplied with your hardware are not identified by gauge number, determine their gauge by matching them against the life-sized drawings of screwheads below. If screws supplied with your hardware are too short for secure fastening, use the bottom row of the chart to help you select longer screws of the same gauge.

Screw gauge	No. 6	No. 7	No. 8	No. 9	No. 10	No. 12	No. 14
Pilot-hole bit	5/64″	3/32″	3/32″	7/64″	7/64″	1/8″	9/64″
Shank-hole bit	9/64″	5/32″	11/64″	3/16″	13/64″	15/64″	1/4″
Lengths available	3/8″-1½″	½″-1½″	½″-2½″	¾″-2½″	¾″-3½″	¾″-3½″	1″-4″

Saw-proofing a Door

Steel bars for the lock area. To shield the lock in a solid-core flush wooden door, bore ¼-inch holes 8 inches deep into the lock-side edge at 2-inch intervals. Use a drill guide, an inexpensive device available at most hardware stores, to keep the holes at a 90° angle to the door edge, and bore with a ¼-inch "bell-hanger" bit 12 inches long. Drilling no closer than 1 inch to the bolt or latch plates, drill five holes above the locks in your door, five holes below them and as many holes between them as possible. To make all holes an equal depth, wrap tape 8½ inches from the tip of the bit. Into each hole, tap a 7½-inch length of unthreaded ¼-inch steel rod, then seal the holes with wood filler.

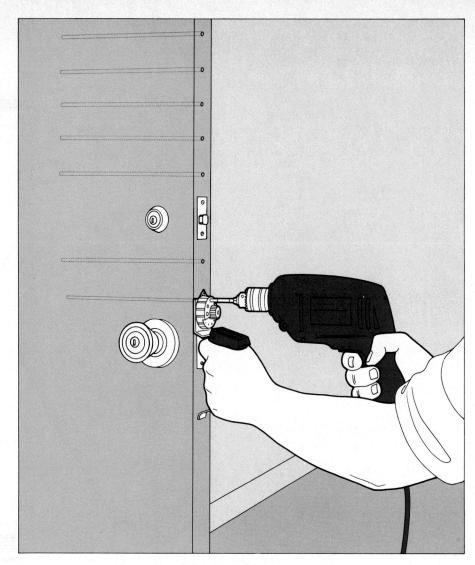

A Strike to Lock a Dead Bolt Right

1 Recessing the strike. Unscrew the old dead-bolt strike plate, use a chisel to enlarge the slot in the jamb to accommodate the box of the new strike, and set the strike in the jamb to check its position; the bolt of the lock must slide into the box without binding. If necessary, enlarge the strike-box slot further and reposition the strike.

To set the dimensions of the new plate recess, trace around the plate, then chisel a recess within the outline so that the strike plate lies flush with the surface of the wood.

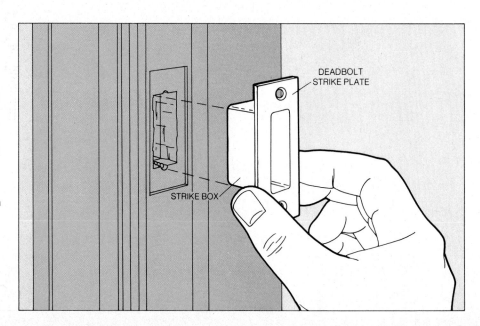

DEADBOLT STRIKE PLATE

STRIKE BOX

2 **Fastening the strike.** With the strike in the jamb, use the screw holes in the strike plate and strike box as guides to bore into the studs beyond the jamb. Drill the holes to fit No. 10 wood screws 3 inches long, using the hole dimensions and drilling method shown on page 21.

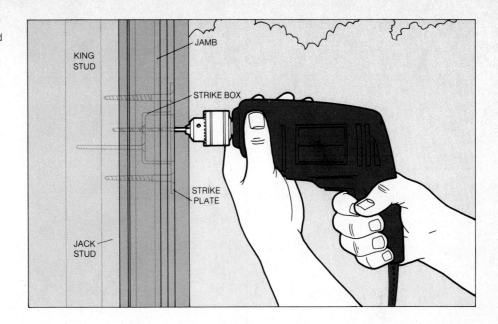

Stiffening a Frame

1 **Removing the side casing.** Unscrew the strikes from the door jamb and remove both side casings with the flat end of a pry bar, working from the bottom of the casing up and using a thin scrap of wood behind the bar to protect the wall. Pull out any nails left in the wall or casings, using carpenter's nippers.

Examine the space between the jambs and the jack studs. If you find no shims at the locations indicated in the inset, proceed to Step 2; if you do find shims, proceed directly to Step 3.

2 **Adding shims.** Secure bracing of a doorjamb requires, at each of the points indicated in the inset of Step 1, 4-by-6-inch fillers of ¼-inch plywood and two pieces of standard door shim, one of which has 3 inches trimmed from its thin end. Insert the plywood filler behind the jamb, leaving space for the thick end of the untrimmed shim. Push the shim into the gap between the filler and the stud, then tap the trimmed shim into the opening, thin end first, until the shims are snug.

Install one shim assembly behind each hinge; behind the dead-bolt strike, use two fillers separated by a gap for the box of a high-security strike (*page 22, bottom*). To secure the fillers, replace short hinge screws with 3-inch strike-plate screws and drive pairs of identical screws above and below the strike plate.

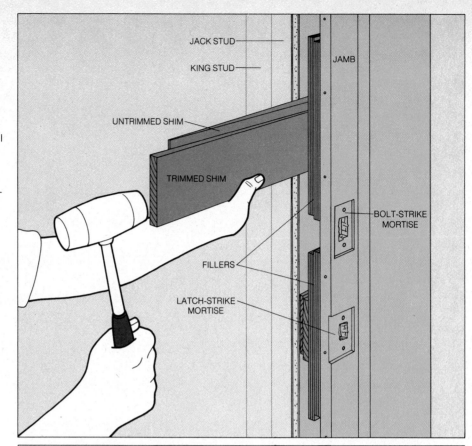

JACK STUD

KING STUD

JAMB

UNTRIMMED SHIM

TRIMMED SHIM

BOLT-STRIKE MORTISE

FILLERS

LATCH-STRIKE MORTISE

3 **Reinstalling the casing.** Nail the side casings to the jambs and the jack studs, from top to bottom, using sixpenny finishing nails in the studs and fourpenny finishing nails in the jambs, reusing old nail holes where feasible. Lock-nail the side casings to the top casing with one sixpenny nail driven vertically and another driven horizontally into each mitered joint.

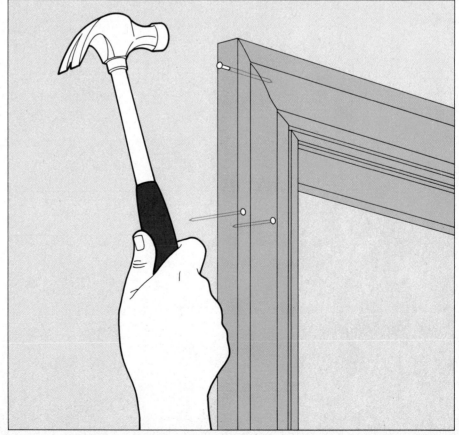

Securing Problem Doors

Pinning exterior hinges. If your door swings out instead of in, remove a pair of screws from each hinge—one from the jamb leaf and a second, opposite the first, from the door leaf. Hammer 20-penny nails into the empty screw holes in the jamb leaves, leaving ½ inch of each nail protruding from the leaf. Cut off the nail heads with a hacksaw.

Keeping a sliding door in its tracks. Open the door and drill holes at 10-inch intervals in the overhead track with an $^{11}\!/_{64}$-inch bit. Drive a 1½-inch No. 12 sheet-metal screw into each hole, allowing the screwheads to protrude enough to prevent the door from being lifted out of its tracks but not so far that they will rub the door as it is opened and closed (*inset*).

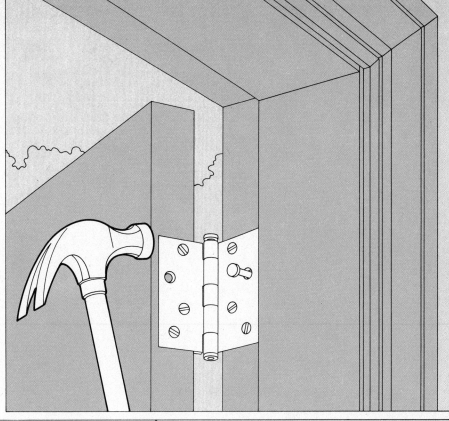

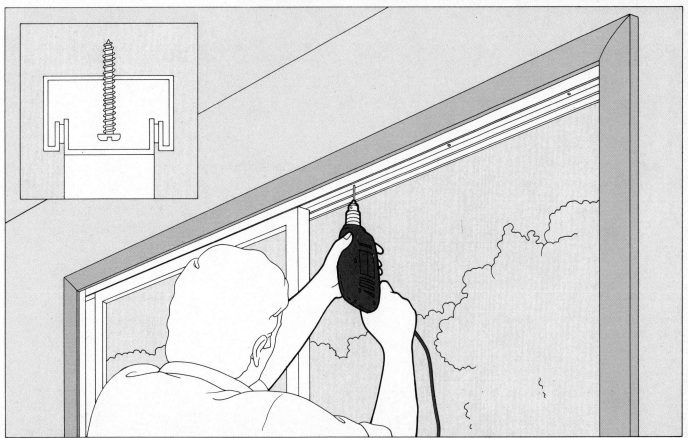

Barring the Door: The Basic Locks and Bolts

Modern door locks operate on a simple and ancient principle. A rigid locking arm, called a bolt, is mounted in or on the door so that it can be slid into a socket, or strike, attached to the doorframe. There are two types in wide use today: the spring-latch and the dead-bolt. The spring-latch *(opposite, center)*—sometimes called a key-in-knob lock—is the more convenient. Its locking arm, or latch, is activated by a spring mechanism and engages automatically as the door is closed. There may also be a plunger that locks the latch in place.

A key-in-knob lock offers poor security, for a burglar can pop the latch out of the strike. The dead-bolt lock offers better protection because its bolt does not work automatically, but must be opened and closed by a thumb turn or a key. Such a lock generally is installed in addition to one of the spring-latch type. For a door containing glass, a double-cylinder dead-bolt should be used: it is operated on both sides by a key, preventing a burglar from reaching through a broken windowpane to open the door.

The simplest dead-bolt is a rim lock *(opposite, top right),* in which the lock and a set of strike rings are fully exposed on the inside faces of door and frame. Rim locks normally come with short installation screws that are vulnerable to prying. To make these locks more secure install them as shown on pages 34-35.

Far stronger than any rim lock is a dead-bolt that is mounted inside a door and locks into a strike box inside the doorjamb *(opposite, bottom left).* A mortise lock *(opposite, bottom right)* combines a dead bolt and a spring latch in a single handsome—and expensive—unit but is difficult to install. Do not try to put one in unless you are sure you can master the technique shown on pages 35-36.

Even stronger locking systems *(page 28)* are designed for areas where extreme security is a necessity. These special locks include multiple steel bars that lock into strike plates on both sides of the door, and diagonal bars braced against a door from a socket in the floor.

Sliding doors, garage and shed doors, and French doors call for different measures. A strong padlock suffices on most garages, and a shed needs only a hasp and padlock *(page 29).* Sliding doors can be locked with a metal bar braced between the frame and the sliding panel, or with a lock that pins movable and stationary panels together *(page 29).*

French doors pose special problems. Whichever door is less often opened should be secured to the floor and the top jamb with thumb-activated bolts recessed into the edge of the door. The other door should have a double-cylinder dead-bolt lock.

When buying any kind of keyed lock, ask for the five-pin cylinder type *(below),* which gets its name from the row of five locking pins the key must line up before it can turn to move bolt or latch. Also check the wood screws that come with the lock. Many are too short for secure attachment. Most intruders gain entry by force rather than by lock-picking, and even the best lock has little value unless it is firmly installed in a strong door and frame *(pages 20-24).*

The Intricate Innards of a Five-Pin Cylinder

Modern cylinder-lock mechanisms are a product of a 3,000-year effort to fashion mechanical puzzles that will thwart intruders. Hidden springs, pins, cylinders and shafts are so arranged within a lock that only someone with the puzzle's solution—the correct key—can align the parts and operate the lock.

The lock most widely used today contains sets of pins and springs in two cylinders—a smaller cylinder, called the plug, that fits within a larger cylinder, the shell. The plug and shell have rows of holes—at least five in the best locks—that line up when the bolt or latch is fully locked *(right, top).* In each hole of the shell, a spring pushes against two pins—one from the shell atop one in the plug—forcing them down so that the shell pin enters the corresponding hole in the plug, engaging the plug to keep it from turning.

A notched key lifts both of the pins in each hole *(right, bottom)* so that the separation between the shell pin and the plug pin in each hole coincides with the narrow space—called the shear line—between the plug and the shell. With the solid pins that engage the two cylinders pushed out of the way, the key can rotate the plug and move the drive bar, activating the latch or bolt.

A five-pin lock is difficult to pick, but lockmakers have devised even more intricate puzzles to stump the expert criminal. One manufacturer bevels the pins and the key notches so that the key not only raises the pins, but rotates

them; unless each pin is oriented correctly, the plug cannot move. Another puts three rows of pins in each cylinder and three rows of notches on the key.

Other systems, designed mainly for commercial rather than residential use, have no key cylinders. In push-button locks the correct combination of numbered buttons must be depressed before the bolt can be moved. And in a new computerized system, a magnetically coded plastic card is inserted in a scanner; if the code is correct, the computer activates an electromagnet in the strike box that retracts a bar to disengage the bolt.

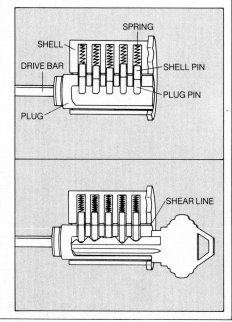

A Guardian for the Front Door

A key-in-knob lock. In this popular model, either of two knobs works the lock: a keyed knob on the outside and an unkeyed inner knob having a thumb turn or button that can immobilize the outside knob. Each of the knobs is connected to a stem that has a semicircular end, and this end is linked to a retractor that connects to the latch and the plunger *(insets)*. As the door—locked or unlocked—is swung shut, the beveled latch and the plunger are pushed back *(upper inset)* by the lip of the strike plate. A ridge in the plunger arm raises the retainer bar, which permits the notch in the latch arm to slide past and retract fully. When the door is completely shut, the latch moves into the strike box, but the plunger does not.

If the inside button is set in the locking position, the latch cannot be forced back because the retracted plunger no longer supports the retainer bar, and the bar will catch the notch in the latch arm. The key or the inside knob can move the unlocking arm to raise the retainer bar and permit the latch to be withdrawn.

The outside knob cannot withdraw the locked latch because a pin attached to the locking button engages a notch in the stem of the outside knob, immobilizing that knob. If the inside button is set to the unlocked position, the pin is disengaged from the outside-knob stem; then either the inside or the outside knob can be turned to withdraw the latch, allowing the door to open.

A rim lock. The case of this lock, mounted on the inside of the door, aligns with a strike plate attached to the doorframe. A key from outside and a thumb turn inside operate the lock by turning a drive bar fitted to a catch that raises or lowers a plate encasing the two vertical bolts, which slide into rings in the strike.

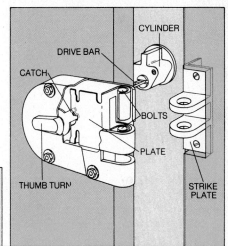

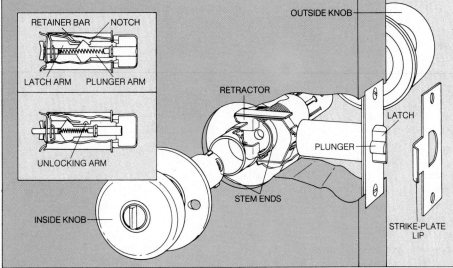

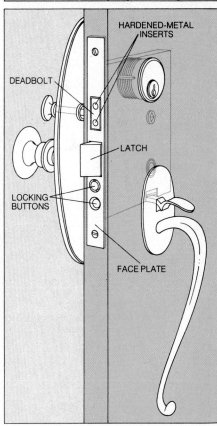

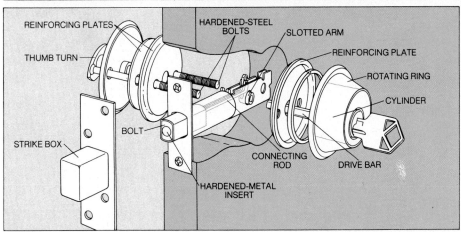

A dead-bolt lock. A key from the outside and either a key or a thumb turn from the inside rotate a drive bar that fits into a slotted arm in the bolt assembly. When the drive bar turns, the arm pulls or pushes a connecting rod to move the bolt into or out of the strike box. In a good dead-bolt lock, the bolt projects 1 inch or more from the door edge and is made of hardened metal or has hardened-metal inserts to resist sawing. The cylinder is secured by hardened-steel bolts. Reinforcing plates and rings prevent the cylinder and bolts from being pulled out of the door; a beveled rotating ring, difficult to grip or crush, circles the face of the cylinder.

A mortise lock. This versatile lock combines a spring latch and a dead bolt in a single unit that fits into a large cutout, or mortise, in the edge of the door. The bolt is locked with a key. A button in the faceplate on the edge of the door immobilizes the thumbpiece, which operates the latch. A second button frees the thumbpiece.

A double-bar lock. This high-security lock, designed mainly for doors that open outward, utilizes the strength of long steel bars that run horizontally along the inside face of the door and slide into strike plates anchored to the vertical studs on each side of the door. The bolts are secured to the door with brackets and are moved by a rack-and-pinion mechanism that is operated by an exterior keylock and an inside thumb turn set in the center of the door.

Protection for Special Doors

Bolts for a French door. On one half of a pair of French doors, vertical bolts in the top and bottom edges of the door lock into strikes in the threshold (*below*) and top jamb. The bolts cannot be dislodged by force, or unlocked through a broken pane of glass. The other half is fitted with a double-cylinder dead-bolt lock.

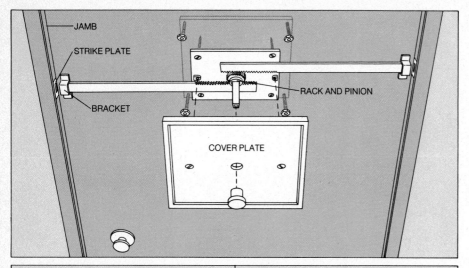

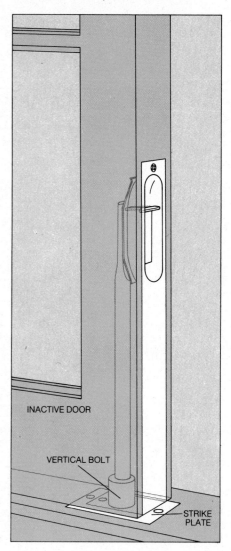

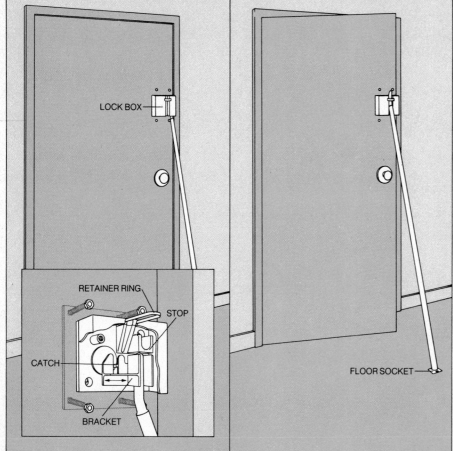

A diagonal-bar lock. This lock, designed for inward-opening doors, has a steel brace between a floor socket and a lock box above the doorknob. The upper end of the brace is secured in the box by a stop and bracket (*inset*). A key from the outside moves a catch that pushes the bracket sideways (*arrows*). The bar then can slide upward through a U-shaped retainer ring, permitting the door to be opened far enough for a hand to lift the bar from the floor socket.

Two ways to lock sliding doors. A pivoted metal bar drops from the doorframe to a socket on the edge of the sliding panel to lock this door securely in place *(top)*. A pin across the socket holds the bar in position and is pulled out to open the lock. When not needed, the bar swings up into a bracket on the doorframe.

For greater security a keyed dead bolt at the base of the doors *(bottom)* locks the sliding and stationary panels together, so that the sliding panel cannot be slid open nor lifted out of its frame. (For another way to block lifting of the movable panel, see page 25, bottom right.)

Padlocks and hasps. A good padlock has a hardened-steel shackle, a lock case of solid brass or laminated steel, and a five-pin cylinder *(page 26)*. The cylinder turns a rectangular drive bar to retract the bolts from notches in the shackle *(inset)*. The shackle then pops up, propelled by a spring near the lock base. In locking, a downward thrust on the shackle forces the beveled bolts back until the shackle notches can engage them.

The ring of the hasp, called a staple, should be hardened steel. The hasp edges should be beveled to ward off prying attacks.

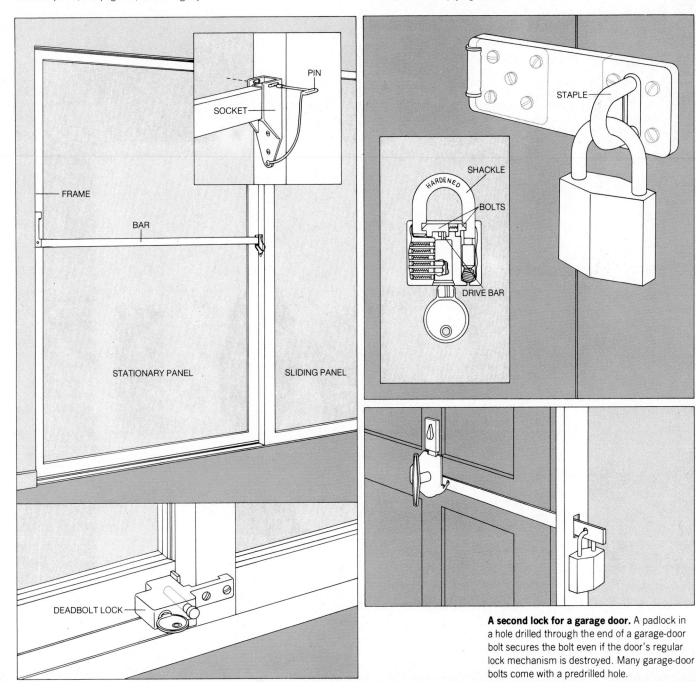

FRAME

SOCKET

PIN

BAR

STATIONARY PANEL

SLIDING PANEL

DEADBOLT LOCK

STAPLE

SHACKLE

HARDENED

BOLTS

DRIVE BAR

A second lock for a garage door. A padlock in a hole drilled through the end of a garage-door bolt secures the bolt even if the door's regular lock mechanism is destroyed. Many garage-door bolts come with a predrilled hole.

Putting On a Better Lock

Some improvements in the locks on your exterior doors can be very simple, involving nothing beyond a change in keys. Others require the addition of new locks or, if you want to use a mortise lock, a brand-new door. For all lock installations except the simplest, careful and precise carpentry is essential, but it is greatly simplified by the use of a special drilling guide; installing a mortise lock demands a very high degree of skill.

First, make maximum use of the good locks you already have. If keys have been lost, have the cylinders rekeyed, a job that a locksmith can do in minutes in his shop. If the existing cylinders are not of the comparatively tamperproof type described on page 26, they ought to be replaced. Either rekeying or replacing a cylinder will require disassembling the lock. In dead-bolt locks, you can free the cylinder entirely; in many key-in-knob locks you will have to stop when you free the outside knob from the lock body and take the knob, with the cylinder still inside, to a locksmith.

The work involved in installing new locks depends on the lock. A rim lock, a dead-bolt lock or a double-door vertical bolt generally can be added to a door without making any changes to the locks already in place. If you replace an existing built-in lock, get an identical model, which will fit into the old holes; otherwise you may have to replace the door.

Before you buy a built-in lock, make sure the door will accommodate it; the door must be thick enough for the bolt mechanism. In a panel door, the vertical edge piece, called a stile, must be wide enough for the knobs of the lock and their decorative rings, called roses. When installing a mortise lock, which requires a new door, be sure the stile is wide enough so that the mortise will not weaken the joint between the stile and the connecting horizontal piece, or rail.

If you plan to use a lock with a beveled latch—a key-in-knob lock, a mortise lock or some models of rim locks—study the way your door swings, for the lock salesman will need to know the "hand" of the door. If, like most exterior doors, your door opens inward, stand outside the house and look at the hinges: a door with hinges on the right side is a right-hand door; one with hinges on the left side is a left-hand door. If your door opens outward, be sure to tell the salesman; such a door often takes a lock that is normally installed on a door of the opposite hand.

Make sure the lock you buy includes all the necessary parts. One is a paper template, a guide that can be folded along a dotted line to fit over the edge and face of the door; the folded template is taped to the door, then pierced at specified points with an awl or nail to locate the holes for the lock. Check the screws that come with your lock and replace any that are too short for good security (pages 20-21); if you are installing a rim lock, replace the mounting screws for its case with carriage bolts and nuts (pages 34-35).

Replacing Cylinders

A spring-latch lock. If screws secure the interior rose, remove them; if none are visible, use the tip of a screwdriver to depress the small metal tab projecting through a slot behind the knob. Pull the knob from the knob stem, push in the spring clip that protrudes from the rose and insert a screwdriver into the notch at the rim of the rose to pry away the rose. Remove the two screws in the mounting plate under the rose and, from the exterior side of the door, pull the outside knob, which contains the lock cylinder.

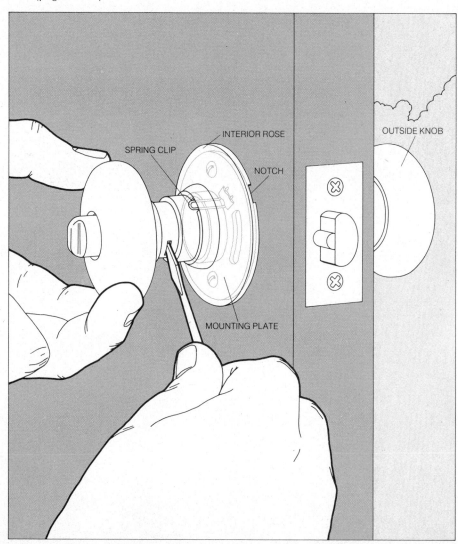

A rim lock. With the door unlocked, remove the screws or nuts that secure the lock case (*below, left*). Wiggle the case off the door and the cylinder drive bar; then remove the screws of the reinforcing plate (*below, right*) and, from outside the door, pull out the cylinder.

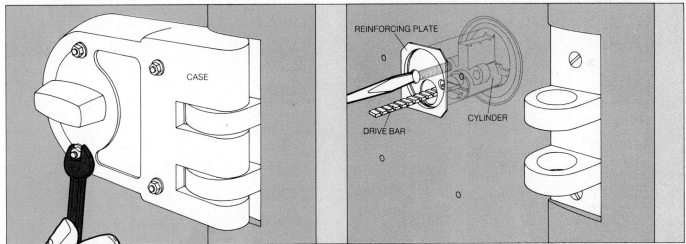

A dead-bolt lock. Take out the screws that secure the interior rose and remove the rose to expose the reinforcing plate; remove the screws holding the plate to free the cylinder. If the lock has no reinforcing plate, simply removing the interior rose will free the cylinder.

On a double-cylinder lock with both interior and exterior cylinders, loosen the screws that extend through the inside cylinder to free both cylinders. If these screws are nonreversible or if they have been deliberately damaged so they cannot be removed, you will probably need a locksmith to remove the cylinder.

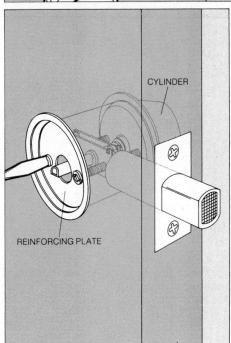

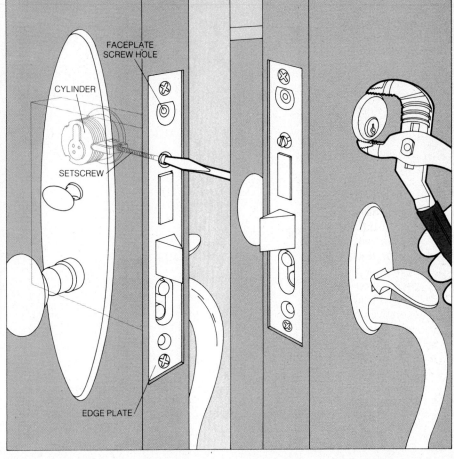

A mortise lock. Find the small setscrew on the edge plate of the door, at the same height as the lock cylinder—if necessary, remove a decorative faceplate from the edge plate to expose the setscrew—and back the setscrew out three or four turns (*left*). From outside the door, unscrew the cylinder; if it does not turn easily, grip its edge with channel-joint pliers, covering the teeth of the pliers with tape to prevent them from marring the cylinder (*right*).

Adding a Dead Bolt

1 Marking the holes. For maximum precision in boring straight, correctly placed holes, start each one by driving a finishing nail straight in ¼ inch through the marks on the paper template, which is taped to the edge and face of the door about 6 inches above the knob. To allow for variations in door thickness, some templates are marked with alternative locations for drilling the edge holes; be sure to use the mark specified for the size of your door.

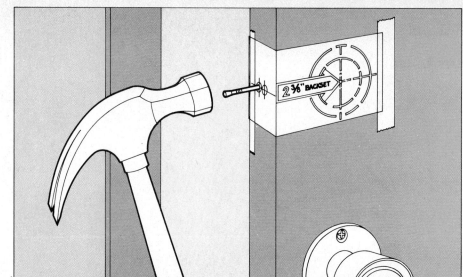

2 Boring the cylinder hole. With the door closed, or firmly wedged open, use a hole saw to bore a cylinder hole the size specified by the manufacturer. To avoid splintering the door face—on a flush door the veneer is very easily damaged—stop drilling as soon as the small bit of the saw breaks through; complete the hole from the opposite side of the door.

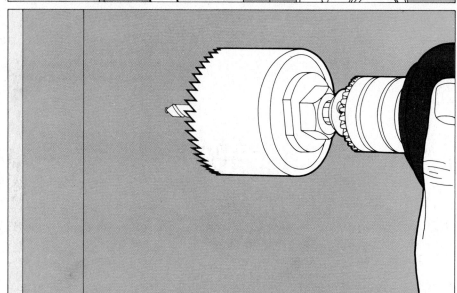

3 Drilling the bolthole. Wedge the door open with a shim. To help keep the drill bit level and straight when drilling the bolthole into the relatively narrow edge of the door, enlist a helper to guide you. While you watch the bit from above to direct it right or left, have your helper kneel so that his eye is level with the hole and he can tell when the bit wanders from true horizontal.

4 **Seating the bolt assembly.** Insert the bolt assembly into the bolthole and use a utility knife to scribe the outline of the faceplate—the score line left by a sharp knife is thinner and more precise than a pencil line. Chisel a mortise in the marked area for the faceplate and fasten the assembly in place with screws.

5 **Installing the lock.** For a dead-bolt with a thumb turn (*right*), assemble the cylinder, the drive bar and the reinforcing plate and ring as directed by the manufacturer. Then fit the assembly into the cylinder hole from outside the door, inserting the drive bar through the drive-bar hole in the bolt assembly. Screw the rear reinforcing plate, if any, to the cylinder hole from inside the door, then set the thumb turn against the door, fitting the drive bar into the thumb-turn hole. Insert mounting bolts through the thumb turn, the reinforcing plate and the bolt assembly and screw them into the back of the cylinder. For a double-cylinder lock, fit the drive bars of both cylinders into the drive-bar hole.

Test the dead-bolt action with both the key and the thumb turn. If the bolt will not move in or out, remove the drive bar from the cylinder, rotate the bar 180° and reassemble the lock.

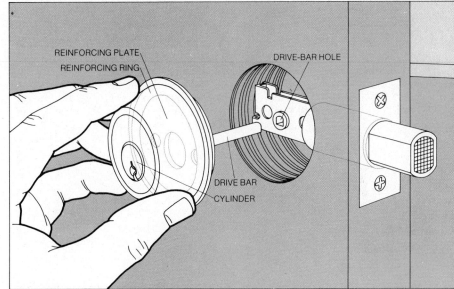

REINFORCING PLATE
REINFORCING RING
DRIVE-BAR HOLE
DRIVE BAR
CYLINDER

6 **Marking for the strike box.** Coat the end of the bolt with lipstick or a grease pencil, close the door and use the thumb turn or key to press the bolt against the jamb, leaving a mark on it. Using the bit with which you bored the bolthole, bore a hole for the strike box into the jamb at the mark. If you hit a finishing nail, chisel around it until you can pull it out with pliers.

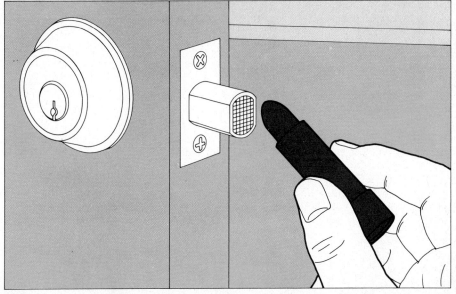

Installing a Spring-Latch

Fitting the lock. Drill a cylinder hole and a bolthole and mortise the latch assembly as for a dead-bolt lock *(pages 32-33, Steps 1-4)*; then from the outside set the lock body in place, engaging the end pieces of the latch assembly *(inset)*. From the inside, screw the inner mounting plate to the lock body. Finally, install the interior rose and knob, reversing the steps described on page 30. Install the strike plate in the same way as a dead-bolt strike.

LATCH ASSEMBLY

Installing a Rim Lock

1 Mounting the lock. About 6 inches above the doorknob, bore a hole for the cylinder. Insert the cylinder from the outside, screw the rear reinforcing plate to it and set the lock case against the door so that the drive bar fits into the thumb-turn slot of the case. If necessary, you can shorten the drive bar by breaking it with pliers at one of the grooves. Bore holes for the attachment bolts, using the lock case to locate the boltholes. Bolt on the lock case, placing lock washers and nuts on the inside.

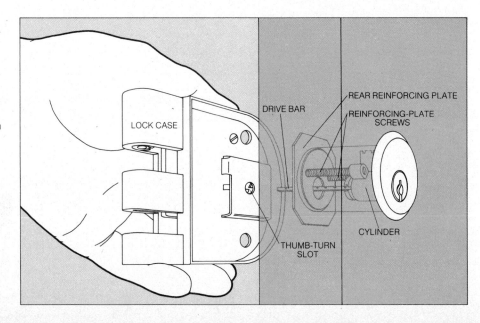

LOCK CASE

DRIVE BAR

REAR REINFORCING PLATE

REINFORCING-PLATE SCREWS

THUMB-TURN SLOT

CYLINDER

2 **Mortising for the strike.** With the door closed, score lines where the top and bottom of the lock case touch the door casing *(below, left)*. With the door open, hold the strike between these marks and score a vertical line in the casing along the outer edge of the strike *(below, right)*; mark a second line one strike-thickness far- ther out in the casing *(dotted line)*. Tap a chisel, bevel side in, along the outermost marks to cut straight into the casing; then, holding the chis- el bevel side down, pare out the wood within the marked area, taking care not to dig in too deeply. For the jamb mortise, hold the strike in the casing mortise, mark around the strike and chisel out a recess in the jamb in the same way the mortise in the casing was cut.

Test the strike mortises as you chisel re- cesses, paring away wood until the lock bolts slip easily into the rings of the strike. If you mortise too deeply, shim behind the strike with cardboard.

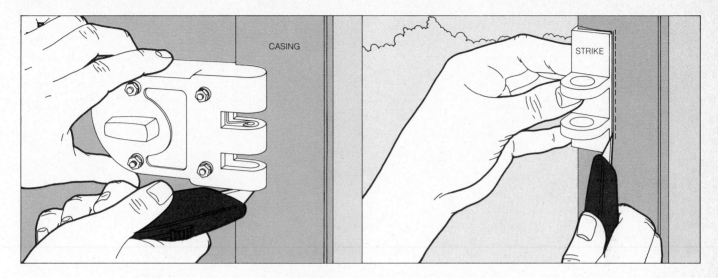

Installing a Mortise Lock

1 **Starting the mortise.** This lock fits inside a deep mortise in the thin edge of the door and re- quires precision work best done with a special guide *(page 37)*. Use the manufacturer's tem- plate to locate the knob and cylinder holes and to outline the mortise, then use a spade bit as wide as the mortise to mark a string of holes down the mortise, spacing the top and bottom marks for adjoining holes about ¼ inch *(right)*. Use the bit and drill guide, set to the depth of the mortise, to drill the holes.

Do not drill for a mortise lock, even with a helper to direct your bit, unless you are certain of your skill—a bit that wanders even slightly could ruin an expensive door.

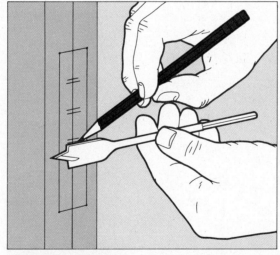

2 **Chiseling the mortises.** Chip the remaining wood out of the mortise with a chisel and mallet, making many small cuts rather than a few large ones, to keep the chisel from biting too deeply. At the last stage of the job, keep the beveled side of the chisel facing into the mortise and shave the walls flat without a mallet.

Drill the holes for the thumbpieces, knob and cylinder, taking care to drill all the way into the mortise. Set the lock into the mortise and, holding it straight up and down along the edge of the door, mark the shallow faceplate mortise *(page 33, Step 4)*. Chisel out the faceplate mor- tise and screw in the lock.

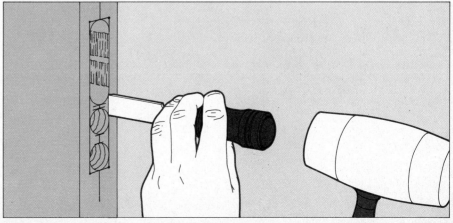

3 **Installing the cylinder and trim.** From outside, screw the threaded cylinder into the lock case and secure it with the setscrew, which runs from the edge plate into the lock. Attach the outside thumbpiece or knob, the inside thumb turn and knob, and the trim. Install the strike as you would for a dead bolt *(page 33, Step 6)*.

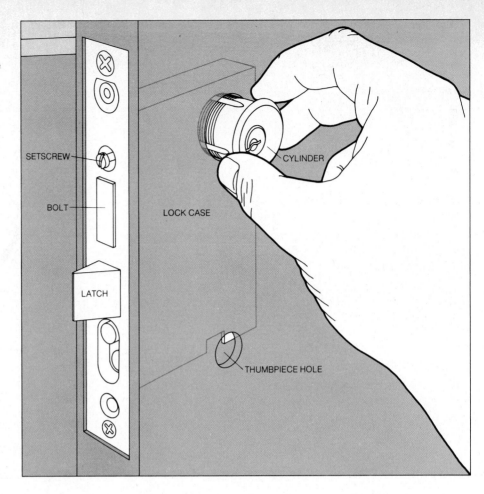

SETSCREW

BOLT

LOCK CASE

CYLINDER

LATCH

THUMBPIECE HOLE

Vertical Bolts for a French Door

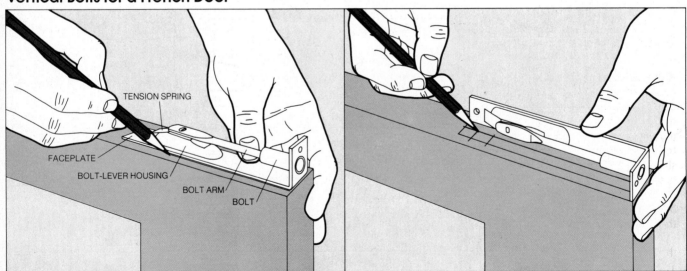

TENSION SPRING

FACEPLATE

BOLT-LEVER HOUSING

BOLT ARM

BOLT

1 **Marking for the mortise.** Remove the inactive door—the door that is usually closed—from its hinges, center the bolt assembly face down on the edge of the door, flush with the top, and trace the outline of the faceplate to indicate the area of the main mortise *(left)*. Draw a center line through this area, parallel to the door edge, lay the bolt assembly on its side *(right)* and mark across the mortise area at the end of the bolt-arm tension spring, at the end of the bolt arm and at the point where the bolt arm engages the bolt. In addition, mark the position of the bolt-lever housing. The marks will serve as guides for cutting the lock-assembly mortise.

2 **Making the mortise.** Using the marks you have drawn as guides, chisel the mortise to accommodate the tension spring, bolt-lever housing, bolt arm and bolt. For each mortise section, use a chisel that is as wide as the corresponding part of the assembly and cut each section only as deep as necessary for fit. Mortise the door edge and top for the faceplate, then screw the assembly in place. Repeat Steps 1 and 2 at the bottom of the door, then rehang the door and install strike plates in the top jamb and in the threshold (*page 33, Step 6*).

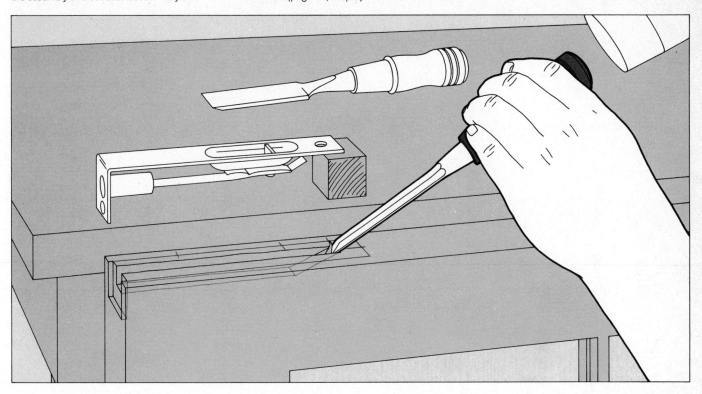

A Guide that Takes the Guesswork out of Drilling

A drill guide, which resembles its larger cousin the drill press, offers a sure way of drilling a hole straight and perpendicular—even into a door edge. The model shown here consists of a bracket to hold the drill, a pair of runners that slide along two steel rods, and a round base. When the guide is to be used, the chuck is unscrewed from the drill, the bracket is attached to the drill shaft, then the chuck is put back on.

When the rod ends are set flush with the base, the drill guide can be used on a door face; with the rods pushed partway through the base *(right)*, the guide can steady a drill bit on a door edge. A lock collar on one rod can be set to stop the drill when the bit has reached a predetermined depth.

To use a drill guide, hold the base

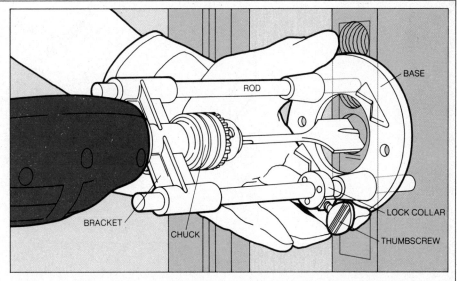

against a door edge with one hand pressing the rods against the faces of the door. Since most doors have a beveled edge, hold the rods tight against the faces of the door; one side of the

base plate then will ride about ⅛ inch above the beveled corner of the door. Use your other hand to operate the drill. The drill's torque will help lock the guide rods against the door faces.

Windows that Cannot Be Jimmied or Smashed

Even a novice burglar generally knows how to unlatch a window with a knife blade inserted between the window sashes. And unless a window is fitted with special break-resistant plastic panes *(page 40)*, it is relatively simple to cut or break away enough glass to reach inside and undo the latch. However, any of a number of locking devices can guard windows against all but a skilled and persistent intruder. Some of them are clearly visible additions, and thus are useful as deterrents. The sight of a formidable-looking lock can persuade a criminal to move on and try his luck elsewhere.

Ideally, every window easily accessible from outside should be fitted with a lock, but any window that might become an emergency exit in a fire should be locked in such a way that it can be opened quickly and easily from inside. Locks that work with a key should be keyed alike, so that one key will open any window, and a key should be kept where it is handy

for use from inside but cannot be fished for from outside.

For the common double-hung window—two wooden sashes that slide up and down in a frame—the simplest lock to install is a keyed unit that replaces the standard thumb latch. Sometimes you will not even have to drill new holes to do the job. But to prevent an intruder from unscrewing this type of lock—or any other that is anchored with common screws—you should deface the heads of the screws that come with the lock or fasten it with nonretractable "prison" screws *(below, left)*.

The keyed latch is also, unfortunately, one of the least effective window locks; it is readily loosened from outside with a pry bar. More effective locks rely on a metal shaft that pierces both sashes *(opposite, top)* and holds them tightly together. Mounted near the side of the window rather than in the middle, such locks are relatively pry-resistant. Another

advantage of this kind of lock is that it can secure a window in two positions—closed or partly open for ventilation.

The same dual feature is offered by a wedge-type lock *(opposite, bottom left)*, which comes with two strike plates for the open and shut positions. Locked into the top sash and holding the bottom sash down with a toothed wedge, the lock is a highly effective barrier against break-ins.

More difficult to lock than conventional double-hung windows are horizontally sliding glass windows and casement windows. Sliding glass models are best secured by the methods that are used for sliding doors *(page 29)*. In a casement window that opens with a crank, you can simply remove the crank handle from the shaft and put it at a location near the window but out of a burglar's sight and reach. For extra protection, however, you can replace the standard latch with a latch that must be locked with a key *(opposite, bottom right)*.

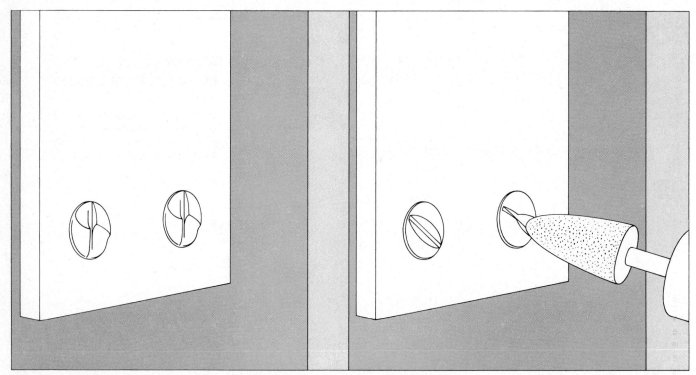

Putting in screws for keeps. A nonretractable screw *(left)* has a special head, making the screw impossible to remove without destroying screw or framing. Before tightening such screws, be certain that the lock you are fastening is positioned correctly. If nonretractable screws are not readily available, use the tip of a conical grindstone in an electric drill to erase the screw slot *(right)*. Grind only along the sides of the slot; excessive grinding can weaken the screw.

Locks for Double-hung Windows

Locking a window with a nail. Drill a ³/₁₆-inch hole through the top rail of the bottom sash and into the bottom rail of the top sash. Angle the hole slightly downward so that the nail cannot fall out if the window is rattled and drill it at least ½ inch into the top sash. Trim the head from a 10-penny common nail with wire cutters so that the nail is just out of reach when slipped into the hole. Keep a magnet near the window to retrieve the nail and unlock the window.

Installing a lag-bolt lock. Close the top and bottom sashes, then drill a ¼-inch hole through the bottom sash and about halfway into the top sash. Position the hole about ½ inch from the window frame and the top of the bottom sash to miss the glass. Enlarge the first ¼ inch of the hole with a ⅝-inch bit for the metal shield at the head of the lag bolt. Then slip the shield onto the bolt and screw it in place with the wrench provided by the manufacturer.

Fitting a rod lock. Hold the body of the lock against the top rail of the bottom sash to locate a rod hole that misses the glass in both sashes. Mark holes for rod and mounting screws with an awl and drill them. Use a ¼-inch bit, taped for a hole about 2⅜ inches deep, for the rod. Screw the lock body to the sash. To allow ventilation, open the bottom sash no more than 4 inches and insert the rod in the lock to mark the top sash for a second rod hole about ½ inch deep.

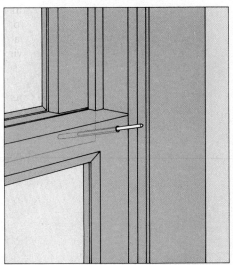

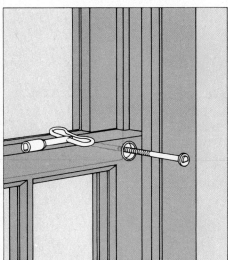

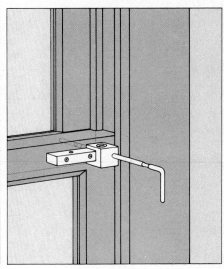

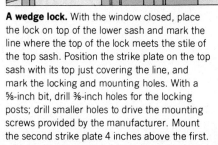

A wedge lock. With the window closed, place the lock on top of the lower sash and mark the line where the top of the lock meets the stile of the top sash. Position the strike plate on the top sash with its top just covering the line, and mark the locking and mounting holes. With a ⅝-inch bit, drill ⅜-inch holes for the locking posts; drill smaller holes to drive the mounting screws provided by the manufacturer. Mount the second strike plate 4 inches above the first.

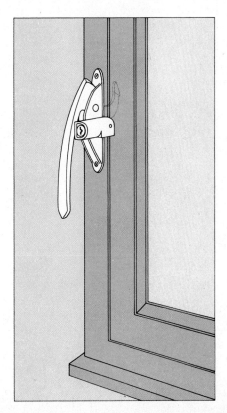

A Keyed Latch in a Casement Window

Installing a locking latch. Open the old latch and unscrew it from the window frame. Fit the new one into the slot in the frame and fasten it with nonretractable sheet-metal screws.

Locking latches are made to fit most metal casement windows; when purchasing the latch, however, specify whether it is to fit on the left or the right side of the window.

Panes of Shatterproof Plastic

Unprotected glass in a window or door is a virtual invitation to a determined burglar. In a matter of seconds he can break the pane, reach inside and open his way in. To foil such a break-in, you can replace the glass with clear plastic. Two types offer different degrees of security.

Acrylic plastic (often referred to by one of its trade names, Plexiglas) generally will stop a thrown rock but will break if attacked with a hammer. It is generally used in garages and outbuildings, where vandalism is more of a concern than burglary. A much greater degree of protection is offered by polycarbonate resin plastic (often called Lexan, another trade name), which is twice as expensive as the acrylic, but is able to withstand a sledgehammer blow. The only way to get past a pane of polycarbonate is to remove it from the sash in one piece—or to destroy the sash.

Both types of plastic look like glass and have the same optical characteristics, but are much easier to scratch. Superficial scratches can be covered with clear automobile paste wax (do not use a cleaner-wax combination). Deep ones must be sanded out in several steps—preferably with a sequence of 320-, 400- and 600-grit sandpaper—then buffed with a 4-inch muslin wheel. Because of the danger of scratching, leave the protective shipping paper on until the pane is installed. Clean the installed panes with mild detergent and a soft cloth—do not use household cleansers containing ammonia or abrasives—then wipe the surface with a damp cloth to remove static charges that may attract dust particles.

Like glass, sheet plastic is available in several standard sizes and may have to be cut to fit your window frame. Acrylics can be cut with a special scribing tool or sawed with a circular saw having a blade of at least 6 teeth per inch or a saber saw having a blade designed for plastics. The polycarbonates must be cut with a circular saw with a carbide-tipped blade (at least 10 teeth per inch); many suppliers will cut panes to size for you.

The thickness of the plastic sheets corresponds to that of window glass: $1/10$-inch plastic is roughly the same as single-strength, $3/32$-inch glass; $1/8$-inch plastic is the equivalent of double-strength glass.

Stronger sheets, $3/16$ or $1/4$ inch thick, can be used for extra security if the glass channel in a wooden sash is wide enough to accommodate them; in metal frames the new pane must match the old.

Plastics are installed in much the same way as glass, but ordinary glazing compound cannot withstand the thermal expansion and contraction of sheet plastic; use an elastic, silicone-based compound.

To begin an installation job, soften the glazing compound around the old windowpanes with linseed oil, wait 30 minutes and scrape off the compound with a wood chisel; if the compound does not soften, heat it with the top of a soldering iron. On a wooden sash, force the glazier's points away from the pane with a putty knife, pull them out with a pair of long-nose pliers and tilt the pane out of the sash. Clean the channel with a wire brush, then sand and paint it—unlike ordinary glazing compound, the silicone sealant will not bond to bare wood.

To determine the size of the new pane, measure the inside of the sash and subtract $1/16$ inch from each dimension; subtract an additional $1/16$ inch per foot of width or length to allow for thermal expansion, unless you are working in weather hotter than 85° F.

Setting Plastic in a Wooden Sash

1 Cutting the pane to size. Use the square, straight edges of the plastic sheet for two sides of the new pane and mark the other two sides on the plastic's protective paper with a pencil and a framing square. Set the sheet on a workbench, clamp a piece of straight 1-by-4 over it, parallel to the marked line, and cut slowly along the line with a circular saw, using the 1-by-4 as a guide for the shoe of the saw. Peel away 1 inch of the protective paper from each edge of the cut pane and cut away the paper with scissors, taking care not to scratch the pane. On an acrylic pane, finish the edges with sandpaper, using 80 grit, then 220 grit; on both plastics, wash the edges with mild detergent and water or with naphtha.

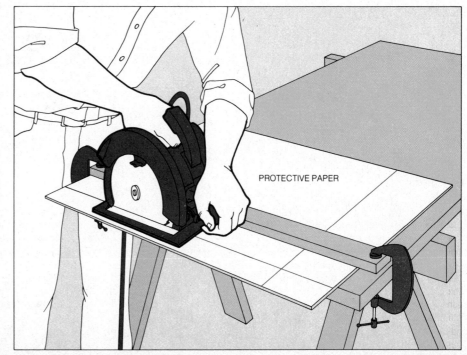

PROTECTIVE PAPER

2 **Installing the pane.** Using a caulking gun, spread a ¼-inch bead of silicone glazing compound around the inside of the sash channels, center the pane in the channels and press it into the compound; then, using a putty knife, press triangular glazier's points into the window frame at 4-inch intervals. Apply a bead of compound around the edges of the pane and, with the putty knife, smooth the bead to a bevel that extends from the face of the pane to the edge of the window sash *(inset)*.

When the sealant has cured for 24 hours, peel the protective paper from both sides of the pane, dissolve the adhesive behind any remaining paper with naphtha and wash the plastic with mild detergent. Do not paint glazing compound.

PROTECTIVE PAPER

Setting Plastic in a Metal Sash

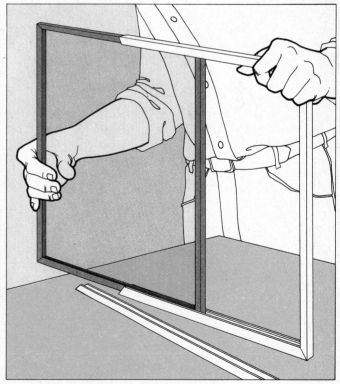

A sash with metal clips. If the edges of the pane are covered by glazing compound, remove the compound, pinch the spring clips that had been hidden underneath it and pull them out of their holes, then tilt the old pane out of the sash. Line the channel with silicone glazing compound, press the new pane into the compound and replace the clips. Cover the clips with compound and bevel it neatly.

A sash with rubber gaskets. If the glass is held by U-shaped rubber gaskets, unscrew one side of the metal sash and pull it off, then slide gaskets and glass out of the sash. Fit the gaskets onto the new pane, slide it into the three sides of the sash and refasten the sidepiece you removed.

Safes and Vaults: Fortresses within the House

For priceless objects and crucially important legal documents, the only adequate safeguard against burglary and fire is a rented safe-deposit box in a bank vault. But most safe-deposit boxes are too small for bulky valuables and too inconvenient for any object or papers you use frequently—silver flatware, cameras, financial records and the like. The best way to protect such items is to store them in a home safe or a burglar- and fire-resistant strong room (page 47).

Before choosing a safe, decide whether you are concerned more about burglary or about fire—protection from both is rarely combined in a single safe. Burglary safes have thick steel bodies, sophisticated combination locks and hardened-steel bolts, but papers inside may char in a fire. A fire safe—cheaper, lighter and more spacious—has a double shell of thin sheet metal filled with several inches of insulation. Some have reinforced doors and combination locks, but these features are only minor deterrents to a thief—a burglar can crack a fire safe in minutes by peeling away the sheet metal.

A fire safe does more than simply block the flow of heat. Its insulation—a crumbly, crystalline mixture of lightweight concrete and granules of vermiculite (a form of mica)—contains as much as 30 quarts of water. Ordinarily the water is locked into the crystal structure. But a fire disrupts the crystals, releasing the water and turning it into steam, in the process absorbing great amounts of heat. The steam, which filters through small vents inside and outside the safe, may crumple and discolor papers, but they will remain legible and flexible enough to handle. Since the water of crystallization is so easily released by heat, old safes may have lost their fire protection; for this reason purchase of a used safe is not recommended.

Look for the Underwriters' Laboratories (UL) label on any fire safe you buy. The label will specify the type of the safe, based on the tests it has passed. An "insulated filing device" will protect papers against the 1,700° F. heat of an intense fire, but may be torn open by falling debris. A "fire-resistant safe" and an "insulated record container" (generally a reinforced filing cabinet) are stronger; they

meet the heat-resisting requirements of the insulated filing device, but will also protect papers from damage received in a collapsing building.

The label will also specify the number of hours the safe will withstand a fire; a 1-hour safe is adequate for home use, although 2- and 4-hour safes are available. And the label will indicate the maximum temperature inside the safe during the course of the fire—Class 350 (350° F.) for a safe designed to protect papers (opposite, top center); Class 150 (150° F.) for a safe designed to protect magnetic tape and photographic transparencies (opposite, top right).

Because the water in the insulation of a fire safe is so easily released, it can make the interior damp. To minimize the problem, locate the safe away from direct sunlight, radiators and other sources of heat, and open it two or three times a week to air the interior. If dampness persists, leave a small bag of silica gel in the safe to absorb moisture, and use airtight plastic bags to seal documents or objects especially susceptible to water damage.

If your safe goes through a fire, locate it as soon as you can safely enter the building and have the firemen wet it with a fine hose spray until it is cool enough to touch. Open the door immediately, while a helper stands by with a fire extinguisher; the contents of the safe may burst into flame when the steam that has been covering them is released. Replace any safe that has been in a fire; its fire resistance is destroyed.

In contrast to a fire safe, which provides absolute protection for a specified period, a burglary safe is an uncertain safeguard, for no safe can resist sophisticated cutting tools. Most home burglary safes can withstand sledge hammers, drills and pry bars for only a few minutes. UL-rated safes, which give better protection, are designed primarily for business use—they weigh 800 pounds or more, and are very expensive. If you buy a safe that does not bear an overall UL rating, evaluate it part by part. It should have a combination lock with a UL label; a UL-listed relocking device, to fasten the bolts automatically if a burglar tries to drill through the lock or punch it out of its housing; a concealed hardened-steel

plate to protect the lock and bolts; and bolts or steel hooks that secure the hinge side of the door.

The style of the safe you buy and the method of its installation depend largely on the construction of your house and the amount of storage space you need. If your house has a concrete floor free of dampness and protected from flooding, you can dig a hole through the floor and pour new concrete around a small in-floor safe (opposite, bottom center). For large objects—a collection of gems or bulky photographic equipment, for example—you may need a steel security cabinet (opposite, bottom right) or even a walk-in strong room (page 47).

Most people choose to get a free-standing safe of moderate size. You must secure such a safe firmly, otherwise a burglar may cart it away. If the safe is to stand on a strong concrete floor, you can increase its weight and strength by having the dealer encase it in a solid concrete block, or by building a shell of concrete blocks around it (page 46). With less labor, you can install the safe in the traditional way, fastening it to a floor or into a false wall (pages 44-45). Use your ingenuity to find locations that will delay or baffle a burglar—for example, set the safe behind a false electrical panel or ventilator, alongside a heating duct, behind the contents of a bookcase or kitchen cabinet, or beneath a stairway.

If you have a centrally controlled alarm system (pages 74-99), you can protect the area around the safe with a motion detector, a floor-mat sensor and a smoke detector to guard against cutting torches. Keep the sensors inconspicuous, so they do not betray the location of the safe; and keep the existence of the safe a secret—remarks by talkative children or neighbors often attract burglars.

The most difficult part of the installation job itself is handling the weight of the safe. With a crew of husky helpers, you can move a small safe with an ordinary appliance dolly, as long as you do not need to use a stairway. If your new safe weighs more than 400 pounds, have the dealer move it for you with hydraulic hand lifts. Many dealers also will arc-weld angle irons or mounting brackets to the safe according to your specifications.

Sure Protection for Valuables

A fire-resistant file. Available in one-, two- and four-drawer sizes, a protective file can hold large objects or large amounts of paper. Inner and outer sheet-metal shells sandwich 2-inch layers of fire-resistant insulation; additional insulation in the front panel of each drawer and in the horizontal partitions between drawers makes each drawer an independent compartment.

A safe for papers. This safe, technically called a Class 350 record safe, has the fire-resistant features of an insulated file but is heavily reinforced to protect documents from falling debris or the collapse of a house and has a UL-approved combination lock to deter burglars. It comes in models that can be mounted in a wall, fastened to the floor or fitted with casters.

A safe for films and stamps. This expensive low-temperature safe—a Class 150 record container—protects objects easily damaged by heat and high humidity. The outer container is built like an ordinary fire safe but an airtight inner container of wood and insulating plastic shields the contents of the safe from steam that is generated by the outer insulation.

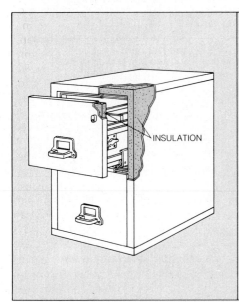

INSULATION

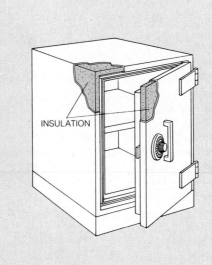

INSULATION

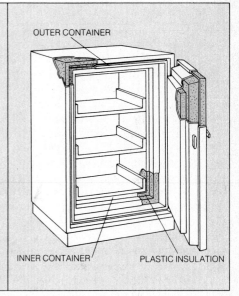

OUTER CONTAINER

INNER CONTAINER

PLASTIC INSULATION

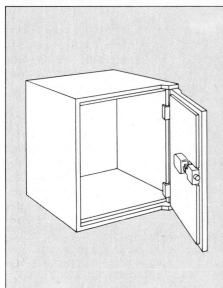

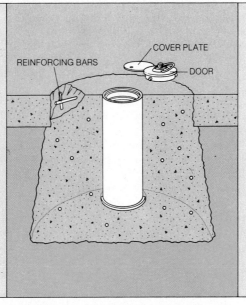

REINFORCING BARS

COVER PLATE

DOOR

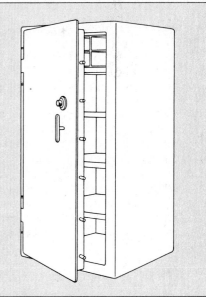

A burglary-resistant wall safe. This 200-pound safe is made of ½-inch steel, with seamless electric welds at all joints. Its door, a steel plate 1 inch thick, is fastened with a sophisticated, three-tumbler combination lock and a hardened-steel bolt; heavy steel hooks interlock with a flange on the body to prevent a burglar from cracking the safe by attacking the hinges.

A safe to bury in the floor. Inexpensive, easy to conceal, fire-resistant and extremely difficult to crack, this type offers advantages that may outweigh its awkward shape and limited capacity. Almost all its strength is built into the 1¾-inch steel door, secured by three 1-inch bolts of hardened steel. The body is protected by a solid block of concrete reinforced with steel bars.

A cabinet for guns and furs. The security cabinet, meant for objects too large to fit inside an ordinary safe, comes in heights up to 80 inches and widths up to 32 inches. The model sketched above is 80 inches high, 30 inches wide and 1,000 pounds in weight. Its body is ¼-inch steel plate, and its ⅜-inch steel door is fastened by 12 steel bolts, six on each side.

Building a Safe into a Wall

1 **Building a false wall.** Cut away the wall covering around the planned location of the safe and, for a safe narrower than the space between studs there, nail horizontal 2-by-4s between the studs of the existing wall, ½ inch above and below the safe location; add cleats under the lower 2-by-4. Mark top and bottom plates for the false wall with stud locations that match the locations of the existing studs. Nail the bottom plate to the floor, spacing it out from the existing wall to accommodate the depth of the safe. Nail studs to the top plate, slide this assembly over the bottom plate, nail the top plate to the ceiling joists and toenail the studs to the bottom plate. Make a cleated 2-by-4 frame in the new wall to match the one in the original wall.

For a safe wider than the stud spacing (*inset*), cut away an existing stud 2 inches above and below the planned location of the new safe and build a frame as described above. Then nail the frame to the cut-off stud and add a vertical 2-by-4 to complete an opening the width of the safe.

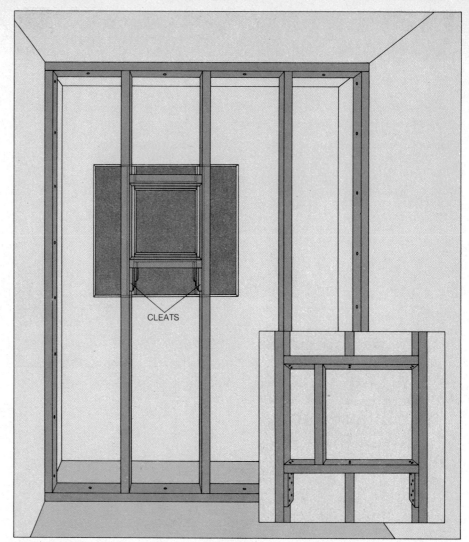

CLEATS

2 **Attaching the mounting brackets.** If your safe does not come with mounting flanges, attach a ¼-by-1½-inch steel angle iron to each side of the safe, ¼ inch farther from the front than the thickness of the wallboard you will use. For a burglary safe (*right*), drill ½-inch holes at 4-inch intervals along the center of each flange of the angle iron and use it as a template to drill matching holes through the sides of the safe. Fasten the angles to the safe with ½-inch carriage bolts, round boltheads facing out. Chisel a ½-inch recess for the angles at the front of the mounting studs to make a flat surface for the wallboard.

On a fire safe install brackets in the same way, but drill ¼-inch holes in the angle flanges that fit against the safe. Drill pilot holes into the sheet-metal shell of the safe—do not drill into the insulation—and secure the flanges with washers and self-tapping sheet-metal screws.

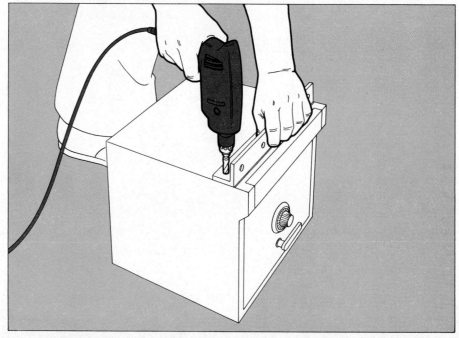

3 **Installing the safe.** With the aid of a helper, slide the safe into the frame, shim the safe until it is level and fasten it to the studs with ½-inch lag bolts 2 inches long. Round the heads of the bolts with a grinder *(page 38)*.

SHIMS

Bolting a Safe to the Floor

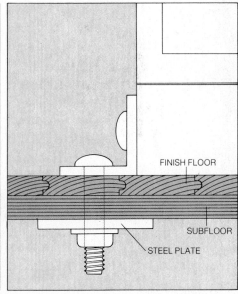

FINISH FLOOR

SUBFLOOR

STEEL PLATE

1 **Marking the holes.** Drill ½-inch holes every 4 inches in two ¼-by-3-inch steel angle irons, set the irons against the skirts at the sides of the safe, and use the angles as templates to mark mounting holes on the skirts and the floor; in addition, mark the corners of the angles on the floor. Tilt the safe onto its back and fasten the angles to the skirt with ½-inch carriage bolts, the round boltheads facing out.

2 **Fastening the safe.** For a wooden floor that is accessible from underneath, drill ½-inch holes at the marks for 3-inch-long carriage bolts and attach the nuts from beneath, using steel plates 3 inches square as washers. If you do not have access to the underside of the floor, use ½-inch lag bolts to fasten the safe to subfloor or joists.

For a concrete floor, use one of the masonry fasteners shown on page 67. Drill pilot holes at least 3 inches deep, using a carbide-tipped masonry bit and a rented hammer-drill, then fasten the safe with machine bolts.

Encasing a Safe in Concrete Blocks

1 **Building the base.** At a corner of the basement floor lay a ¾-inch mortar bed at least 32 inches wider and 8 inches longer than the safe; cover the bed with 6-by-6-inch wire mesh and add another ¾ inch of mortar. Working from the corner, cover the mortar with a course of speed blocks (concrete blocks with built-in channels for reinforcing bars), with ⅜-inch mortar joints between the blocks and between the blocks and the basement wall. For the shorter of the two outer edges of the course, use square-ended corner blocks and make channels in them for reinforcing bars with a hammer and cold chisel. At the shorter inner edge, make a channel running across the blocks.

Lay pieces of ⅜-inch reinforcing bar in the channels of the blocks around all four edges (*inset*). At the corners, use a pipe to bend the ends of the bars to a 90° angle, overlap the bent bars and fasten the overlapping ends with tie wire. Fill the blocks with mortar, troweled off flush with the tops. At the location of the safe, make a platform of broken block cemented with mortar.

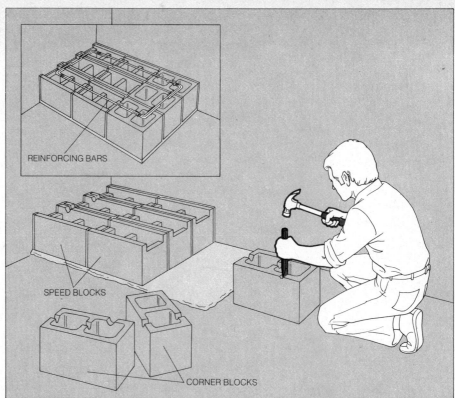

REINFORCING BARS

SPEED BLOCKS

CORNER BLOCKS

2 **Installing the safe.** Bolt vertical angles, each ¼ by 3 inches, to the sides of the safe (*page 44*), 7½ inches in from the front, or have the safe dealer weld them on. With a helper, set the safe on the mortar bed. Lay courses of block behind the safe and along the short edges of the enclosure, with ⅜-inch mortar joints between the courses; fill the gaps between the blocks and the safe with mortar, concrete bricks or concrete half-blocks, depending on the size of the gaps. On top of the safe lay a mortar bed or a course of concrete brick, level with the blocks on each side, then lay a final course of blocks matching the bottom course (*Step 1*), but do not fill the blocks with mortar in this step of the job.

3 **Reinforcing the blocks.** Make a 90° bend at one end of several reinforcing bars and push the bars down through the cores of the outside blocks as far as possible. Lay horizontal reinforcing bars in the channels around the edges of the top course of blocks (*Step 1*). Fill the cores of all the blocks with mortar, then cover the cores with a course of concrete brick.

46

All-around Protection in a Homemade Strong Room

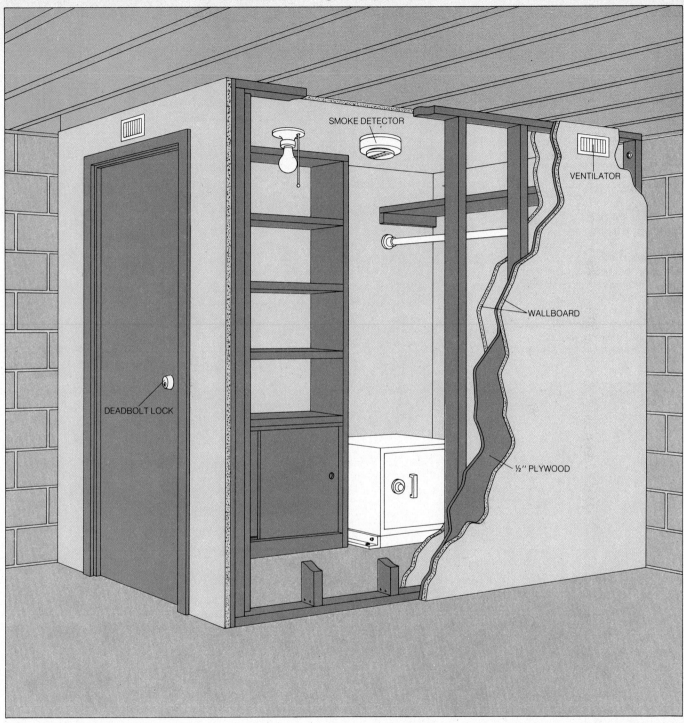

DEADBOLT LOCK

SMOKE DETECTOR

VENTILATOR

WALLBOARD

½" PLYWOOD

Building a strong room. For furs, camera equipment, guns, art objects and the like—and to provide extra protection for a safe—you can build a strong room from scratch in an unfinished basement (*above*) or convert an existing walk-in closet into a strong room. Cover the wall studs (working on the outside of a new room, the inside of an existing closet) with ½-inch plywood nailed every 6 inches. Add a layer of ⅝-inch

Type X wallboard, nailing it every 8 inches (*page 104*) and sheathe the ceiling and the other side of the studs with ⅝-inch wallboard. Install a 1¾-inch solid-core wooden flush door that has been reinforced with steel rods (*page 22*), mounted to swing inward on 4½-inch hinges, and fitted with a dead-bolt lock (*page 32*) as well as a maximum-security strike (*page 22*). Frame holes in two of the walls and install 6-inch-by-8

inch louvered ventilators to prevent moisture from collecting inside the room.

Add a light fixture and some detectors, one inside and one outside the room, wired to a centrally controlled alarm system (*pages 74-99*). A floor-mat sensor outside the room, a perimeter sensor on the door and a motion sensor inside provide maximum burglar protection.

Ironwork: The Art of Security

Architectural ironwork—the metal grilles, railings, fences and gates long valued for their unique combination of beauty and strength—is suddenly back in style after decades of neglect. Old examples are being rescued from the wreckers and painstakingly restored. Craftsmen are making pieces both useful and pleasing to the eye. And artists are creating ironwork as practical as it is sculptural.

Much of this renewed interest can be traced to changes in life style. Security is a major factor; if windows must be barred and yards fenced, protection should be attractive as well as sturdy. There is also the accelerating activity in restoration of gracious old homes—farmhouses, country-town dwellings, and brownstones in central-city districts. The renovators of these neglected dwellings are repairing fences and grilles and scouring junkyards for pieces. But even owners of avant-garde homes, turning from the architectural openness of recent decades, are commissioning ironwork of astonishing beauty and grace.

Coinciding with this desire for more ornament in today's homes is the contemporary crafts movement—the burgeoning production of handmade pottery, cloth, glass and metal pieces individually designed to be both useful and esthetically pleasing. Typical of those taking part in this renaissance is Christopher Ray of Philadelphia, who created the weblike gate on page 55. "I worked as a sculptor of wood for many years," Ray says, "but I always felt confined by the limits of the material. I find that iron allows me to produce works that are spontaneous and expansive and practically unlimited in their form."

Ray and his fellows carry on traditions established by the architects and designers of past centuries. Medieval builders created iron gates as intricately intertwined as the decorative lines in illuminated manuscripts. The forms became simpler as later centuries brought a revival of ancient classicism, but by the mid-19th Century, the elaborate fussiness of the Victorian age took over.

The Victorians were fascinated by the forms that seemingly static metal could take, and the Industrial Revolution enabled them to indulge their fancies. Cheap cast iron, often containing involved designs, could be molded in quantity in a factory rather than hand-wrought by a lone craftsman. Iron was used for almost everything from beds to baby buggies. One catalogue of the day offered fencing by the foot, in a wide variety of patterns; many were advertised as "cheaper than wood."

At the turn of the century, handmade pieces regained popularity. Style was influenced by Art Nouveau, the sinuous lines and fantastic foliate forms most notable in the work of the idiosyncratic Spaniard Antonio Gaudí (page 55). But the Great Depression, which forced builders to cut costs and ornamentation, brought a hiatus ended only by the current architectural-ironwork revival.

Today's wrought iron is not really iron. True wrought iron, which contains a very low percentage of carbon, is no longer produced in the United States. Instead a mild steel is used. It rusts somewhat more readily than iron, but it is worked the same way and looks the same as iron.

Modern technology has altered not only the raw material for ironwork but also the method of fabrication. For most commercial ironwork, bars and rods are joined with welding equipment; simple ornamentation is generally bought ready-made and welded on.

Today's sculptor-ironworker uses these 20th Century techniques, but also relies on traditional smithing methods. He heats the metal in a forge and shapes the malleable material on an anvil. To lengthen a piece, he heats one end to a bright yellow and hammers it, turning the bar 90° with each blow. To make the elongated bar into a scroll, he places it on the edge of his anvil and hits the hot tip from below, curling it like a ribbon. He can also shape the bar cold—twisting it with a clamp or bending it with a jig (page 65).

The smith may use an electric arc and a power grinder as often as he wields the traditional hammer and tongs. But regardless of his tools and techniques, the modern blacksmith's fences, grilles and gates—many of them one-of-a-kind creations—could rightfully be placed on a pedestal instead of on a house.

A potpourri of patterns. Intricate floral scrolls and interlocking squares, diamonds and curves— all popular forms in the fussy Victorian style of ironwork—entwine harmoniously outside this 19th Century home in New York City.

Delicate Patterns for Sturdy Grilles

From the 500-year-old Italian design at right to the examples of 20th Century ironwork on the opposite page, the problems—and the solutions—of making windows secure with grilles have not changed. The pattern of grillwork must let the outside in—allowing for light and ventilation—yet keep outsiders out.

But a well-designed grille does more than fortify an opening. It frames a pleasing view—or obscures an unpleasant one—filters sunlight and creates a fascinating world of shifting shadow patterns. And when the skilled hand and hammer of the blacksmith are fully utilized, window grilles take sculptural forms that, however delicate and whimsical they may appear, are stout guardians.

Quatrefoils and fleurs-de-lis. Quatrefoils—four C-shaped scrolls joined with collars like links in chain-mail armor—are the dominant motif in this 15th Century Venetian window grille. In combination with more ornate fleur-de-lis scrollwork, the quatrefoils form a dense pattern that provides both security and privacy.

Flowers and scrolls. Painted to blend with the façade of the house, this delicate floral grille, crafted in Germany at the turn of the century, melds into its surroundings. Graceful circular scrolls help anchor the framework to the wall.

Pods and leaves. These fanciful curves, which represent seed pods and leaves, are a detail from a contemporary forged-iron grille 11 feet high and 14 feet wide. The grille is bolted to the outer frames of a wide expanse of windows.

Metallic texture. Massive bars make an imposing window grille for a modern Italian residence. Their simple shapes are textured by the fibrous grain of the metal, which complements the rough stone walls.

Railings that Beautify

Many of the railings made for today's homes—whether running alongside a set of stairs or enclosing a balcony—are unimaginative assembly-line creations; however much safer they make a home, they do little to beautify it. That such plain practicality is not inevitable is demonstrated by the ironwork shown here.

Some modern craftsmen forge railings that, like the one at the bottom of the opposite page, add novel twists to the art of architectural ironworking. Others emulate the work of such illustrious predecessors as turn-of-the-century designer Alessandro Mazzucotelli *(bottom)*. Like Mazzucotelli, whose spirals and swirls seem to be in continuous movement, they are creating graceful railings that, in the words of one artisan, "capture the feeling of a fluid arrested in air."

Realistic reproductions. Jutting out from a restored house in Philadelphia, this balcony railing with its heavy, ornate design is typical of the 19th Century fad of reproducing flowers, vegetables, even animals, in iron.

Fantastic foliage. The jutting metal plants on a Milan balcony *(below)*, finished by master ironworker Alessandro Mazzucotelli in 1905, are a hallmark of the Art Nouveau style, which emphasized foliate forms and serpentine curves.

Classic curves. This seemingly fragile stair railing in Milan, Italy, has lasted more than 200 years. The graceful S curves and C curves are held together by welded collars that give the design great strength and stability.

Modernistic figures. A sculpted metal man and automobile (partly visible at top center) are two of the unusual elements worked into the sturdy stair railing below, which adorns a modern building in Bonn, West Germany.

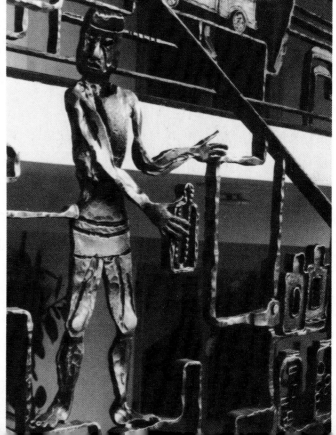

Fences and Gates for Showpieces

Fences and gates, because they are so close to public view, have always fired the imagination of the blacksmith. One of the most inventive ironwork designers was the turn-of-the-century Spanish architect Antonio Gaudí; he is perhaps best known for his surrealistic design for the still uncompleted Church of the Holy Family in Barcelona.

Gaudí came from a long line of coppersmiths. Imbued from childhood with an understanding of the plasticity of hot metal, he used its unusual characteristics to create fluid works of art like the dragon gate opposite, which was inspired by Spanish folklore.

Modern iron sculptors may react to different inspirations, but they follow Gaudí's creative freedom. When Christopher Ray of Philadelphia was asked to produce a contemporary gate that would blend with surrounding colonial ironwork and architecture, he chose the openness of the cobweb design opposite. It achieves, he says, "a strong artistic statement without detracting from its surroundings."

A mail-order motif. The corn-stalk-and-husk design of this 19th Century fence was one of the most popular motifs of the day. Fences in such patterns, which were cast rather than wrought, were sold by the foot and could be ordered from a mail-order catalogue.

A sampler of spears and scrolls. These tall gates in front of a home in Rome contain many common 19th Century designs: curving, spear-like projections, twisting bars, floral scrolls—and two pairs of hammered birds.

A web of protection. A spider and its sturdy web, crafted by sculptor Christopher Ray in 1969, close this passageway into the courtyard of a Philadelphia home. A series of welds holds the web to a heavy frame bolted to the wall.

A master's monster. Its wings and claws part of a gate, this ferocious guardian was designed by Antonio Gaudí in 1885 for a Spanish estate. It depicts a Catalan legend of a dragon that stands watch over an enchanted garden.

Tuning a Torch by the Look of the Flame

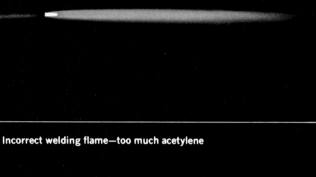

Correct flame for welding

Correct flame for cutting

Incorrect welding flame—too much acetylene

Incorrect cutting flame—too much acetylene

Incorrect welding flame—too much oxygen

Incorrect cutting flame—too much oxygen

Adjusting a welding flame. The correct flame *(top)*, called a neutral flame, is fed by equal amounts of oxygen and acetylene. It burns silently and has a well-defined, rounded white cone at the tip of the torch; when melted by such a flame, steel flows like syrup. If the flame has too much acetylene *(middle)*, the white cone becomes long, pointed and irregular; this flame causes molten steel to boil and leaves a pitted surface. If the flame has too much oxygen *(bottom)*, the flame burns noisily and has a sharply pointed cone; molten steel then sparks badly and develops a surface layer of white foam.

Adjusting a cutting flame. A cutting flame has two components: several small oxy-acetylene flames that heat the steel and a single high-pressure oxygen jet to make the actual cut. With the oxygen jet on, a correct cutting flame *(top)* has well-defined white cones at the tip of the torch and a faint dark area along the cutting jet. If the flame receives too much acetylene *(middle)*, the cones blend into a long, ragged point and the dark area is quite distinct. If the flame receives too much oxygen *(bottom)*, the cones blend into a small square and the length of the flame shortens dramatically.

The Techniques for Welding Steel Grilles

Steel grilles are the traditional and most effective barriers for windows, but this effectiveness is offset by some disadvantages. Inside the house, grilles may block the light and view; outside they are visually obtrusive. For these reasons, grilles generally are used only on basement windows and windows that are hidden from public view. Even in such locations, you should leave one window in each room unbarred, as a fire escape.

Window barriers come in three types. Ready-made, adjustable grilles made of relatively light steel can be simply bolted to the window frame *(page 66)*. With more labor, you can rent equipment and weld together a stronger, more attractive ornamental grille. Or you can bolt lengths of plain ½-inch flat steel horizontally over windows.

Welding—joining pieces of metal by heating them until they melt together—can be done in two ways. In arc welding, an electrical current creates heat by jumping between an electrode and the joint. Arc welds are relatively easy to make, but a machine big enough for a grille needs a 240-volt receptacle.

The other method is gas welding. Oxygen and acetylene from pressurized cylinders are burned at the tip of a torch, melting the metal of the joint. This process requires practice, but it is better suited to home use because it needs no special power supply. Caution is required. Gas welding involves flammable substances; the safety precautions on these pages must be followed carefully.

The tool-rental dealer should provide a set of accessories for the basic welding rig shown at the top of page 58. You will need welding-torch tips for several metal thicknesses, a tip cleaner, steel welding rod (also called filler rod) of several sizes, a T handle for the valve of the acetylene cylinder, tinted goggles and a sparklighter. If any of these items are missing, buy them at a welding-supply shop.

When you rent the welding rig, arrange for the dealer to transport it to and from your home. Locate the rig outdoors at least 25 feet from the house, parked cars, trees, shrubbery and any other combustibles that flying sparks might set afire; place a fire extinguisher nearby and do not allow smoking near the rig.

When welding wear an old, long-sleeved shirt, old pants, leather gloves and leather boots. The pockets of your shirt and pants should have button-down flaps and the pants should not have cuffs; otherwise sparks may catch in your clothes and start a fire. Do not wear hair spray, sweaters or greasy clothes.

Each part of the welding rig requires special precautions. To protect the cylinder valves, the cylinders should always be chained upright on their wheeled truck, never rolled or dragged. Both the torch and the regulators that control the gas pressures are fragile; do not jar or drop them. The regulators should have back-flow check valves *(page 58, top, inset);* if yours do not, install these inexpensive safety valves yourself.

Before you begin welding expensive window-grille stock, practice on scraps of steel *(pages 60-62)* until you can make a smooth, strong weld without brittle pockets of metal oxide. As you work, clean the torch tip frequently *(page 60, Step 6, inset).* You may also need the tip cleaner to determine the size of each tip, using the machinist's-drill number of the cleaner that fits the opening. Some rental dealers provide charts that key the individual manufacturer's tip-numbering system to the thickness of the metal you are welding and the correct filler-rod size.

Whenever the torch is on, be alert for three signs of trouble. If the reading of any regulator gauge creeps upward or does not return to zero when the rig is shut down, the regulator is defective; send the rig back to the supplier.

If the torch sputters or goes out with a loud pop—called a backfire—the torch tip may be clogged; it may be overheated from being held too close to the weld, or the gas pressures may be too low. Let the tip cool, clean it, adjust the working pressures and relight the torch.

If the torch begins making a loud squealing noise, becomes very hot or emits dense smoke, the flame has receded into the torch body or the hoses—a very dangerous condition called a flash-back. Shut off the torch and the acetylene cylinder valve immediately, then close the oxygen cylinder valve. If the hoses are not visibly damaged, take the same steps you would for a backfire and

relight the torch. If either condition persists, return the rig to the supplier.

In the basic grille, vertical pickets—square ½-inch steel bars—fit through holes in two horizontal, U-shaped channels 1 inch wide, called spreaders. Have the steel supplier punch evenly spaced picket holes in the spreaders, no more than 6 inches apart; if you plan to add ready-made ornaments *(page 65, lower right),* match the spacing to their width. If you have a disk grinder, you can buy long lengths of picket and spreader stock, cut them with a cutting torch *(page 63)* and grind the cut ends smooth; otherwise have the supplier cut the steel.

A Safety Checklist

☐ Wear gloves, a plastic face shield and tinted goggles when welding.

☐ If you smell the distinctive, nauseating odor of leaking acetylene, shut down the rig and call the supplier.

☐ Open the acetylene cylinder valve only a half turn and leave the valve wrench in place so the cylinder can be shut off fast in an emergency.

☐ Open the oxygen cylinder valve very slowly—a rush of high-pressure gas can damage the rest of the rig.

☐ Do not use acetylene at a pressure of more than 15 psi—higher pressures can spontaneously explode this gas.

☐ Use pressurized oxygen for welding only—it makes anything it touches extremely flammable.

☐ Never use oil, grease or solvents near the welding rig—they can react explosively with oxygen.

☐ Light the torch with a sparklighter, never with a match—the first puff of flame can burn your hand.

☐ Do not weld or cut galvanized steel or steel plated with zinc, cadmium or lead—they give off toxic gases.

☐ Weld on firebrick, never on concrete, stone or ordinary brick—the heat can explode them. Do not weld directly on a solid firebrick—suspend the work between firebricks.

☐ If the torch squeals loudly, smokes or becomes very hot, shut the acetylene cylinder valve immediately.

Anatomy of a welding rig. The tall cylinder contains oxygen, the short one acetylene; both cylinders are chained to a wheeled truck to prevent tipovers. The valve of the acetylene cylinder is opened by a special T-handled wrench; the oxygen valve is opened by a handwheel. Two regulators (*inset, top*) control the pressure of the gases delivered from the tanks to the torch. A cylinder gauge at each regulator indicates the pressure in the cylinder; the pressure delivered to the torch, controlled by an adjusting screw with a T-shaped handle, is displayed on a working gauge next to the hose connection.

Rubber hoses—red for acetylene, green or black for oxygen—carry gases from the regulators to the torch (*inset, bottom*). The flow of gas from each hose is controlled by a torch needle valve fitted with a small knob. The gases flow through a mixing chamber in the body of the torch, then out a detachable, threaded tip into the air, where the mixture is ignited. A check valve between each regulator and its hose prevents mixed gases from flowing back into the tank.

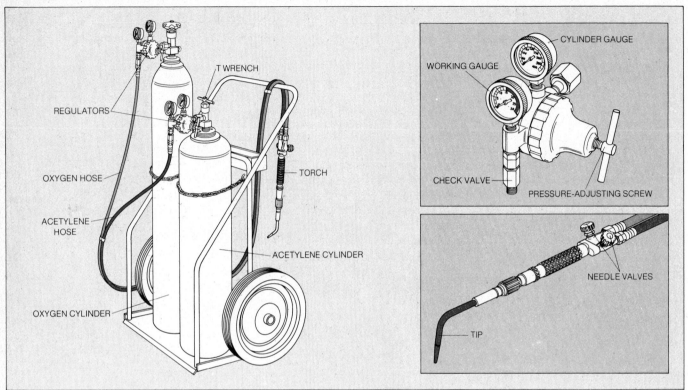

REGULATORS

T WRENCH

OXYGEN HOSE

ACETYLENE HOSE

TORCH

ACETYLENE CYLINDER

OXYGEN CYLINDER

WORKING GAUGE

CYLINDER GAUGE

CHECK VALVE

PRESSURE-ADJUSTING SCREW

NEEDLE VALVES

TIP

Setting Up a Welding Rig

1 Blowing out the nozzles. Remove the protective cap from the acetylene cylinder and wipe out the nozzle with a clean cloth. Point the cylinder nozzle away from yourself and any bystanders and, using a T wrench made for the cylinder, open the valve about a quarter turn for a fraction of a second to blow any dirt from the nozzle. Close the valve immediately. If the valve will not open, replace the protective cap and send the equipment back to the dealer; do not attempt to force the valve open.

Blow out the nozzle of the oxygen cylinder in the same way, using the handwheel on the cylinder. Caution: the oxygen cylinder contains gas under extremely high pressure; make sure no bystanders are within 20 feet and never place your hand in front of the nozzle.

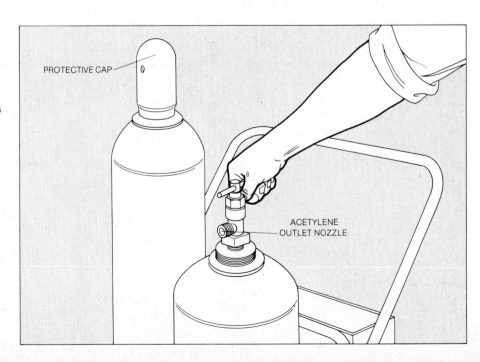

PROTECTIVE CAP

ACETYLENE OUTLET NOZZLE

2 Connecting the regulators. Close the acetylene regulator by turning the adjusting screw
counterclockwise until you feel no resistance.
Fit the regulator onto the nozzle of the acetylene
cylinder and tighten the nut firmly clockwise.
Connect the oxygen regulator in the same way.

Connect the red hose to the check valve of the
acetylene regulator and connect the green or
black hose to the oxygen check valve, then tight-
en the hose nuts. The nuts of the acetylene
hose are marked with a groove and they screw
on counterclockwise; those of the oxygen hose
are unmarked and screw on clockwise.

3 Blowing out the hoses. Slowly open the acetylene
cylinder valve about a quarter turn and leave the
wrench in place. Caution: stand to the side of the
regulator while you open the valve—the pressure
of the gas can blow out a defective regulator
mechanism. Point both hoses away from your
body and any bystanders, and turn the adjusting
screw of the acetylene regulator clockwise about
a quarter turn. When the working-pressure gauge
shows 5 psi (allow a maximum of three seconds),
close the screw and the cylinder valve.

Turn the handwheel on top of the oxygen cylinder
valve counterclockwise very slowly as far as possible, then blow out the oxygen hose. Caution: always open this valve slowly and completely.

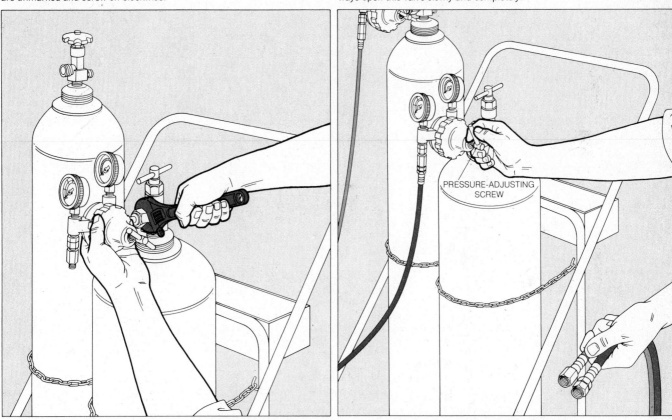

PRESSURE-ADJUSTING
SCREW

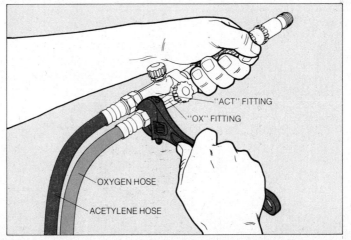

"ACT" FITTING

"OX" FITTING

OXYGEN HOSE

ACETYLENE HOSE

4 Connecting the torch. Fasten the loose end of
the red acetylene hose to the torch fitting marked
ACT or FUEL, turning the hose nut counterclockwise. Connect the green or black oxygen hose to
the torch fitting marked OX or OXYGEN, turning
the hose nut clockwise. Tighten both connections.

5 **Checking for leaks.** Close the torch needle valves and, with the acetylene cylinder valve open a half turn and the oxygen cylinder valve fully open, turn the adjusting screw of each regulator clockwise until the acetylene working-pressure gauge reads 5 psi and the oxygen working-pressure gauge reads 20 psi. Close the cylinder valves. If either cylinder reading drops within five minutes, the system has a leak.

To locate a leak, pressurize the system again (above) and brush a leak-detecting solution—you can buy one, or make one, by mixing a capful of liquid dishwashing detergent into 1 gallon of warm water (do not use soaps containing lanolin or oil)—over all connections and valves and along the hoses. Bubbles will appear at the site of the leak. If a hose or valve leaks, or if a connection leak cannot be stopped by tightening the coupling, shut down the rig (Step 1, below) and notify the supplier immediately.

6 **Attaching the tip.** If your torch has a separate mixing chamber, screw it onto the torch; then screw the welding tip into the mixing chamber. If your torch does not have a separate mixing chamber, screw the tip into the torch body. Do not tighten the chamber or tip with pliers, or change tips while the torch or tip is hot.

Remove any dirt from the tip opening with a tip cleaner (inset). Start with the smallest cleaner that will fit into the opening and follow it with larger cleaners until the opening is clear. Take care not to enlarge the opening or change its shape and never force a cleaner into the opening. Clean the tip whenever dirt builds up inside it during the course of the job.

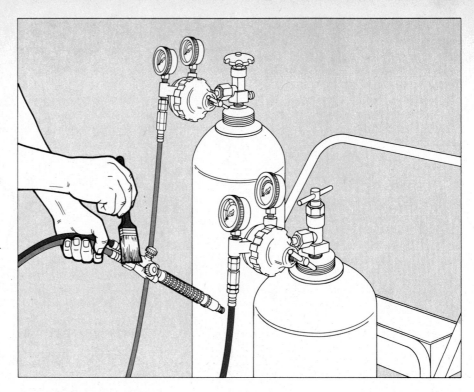

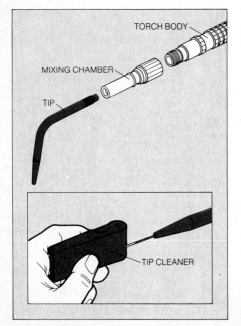

TORCH BODY

MIXING CHAMBER

TIP

TIP CLEANER

The Art of Puddling

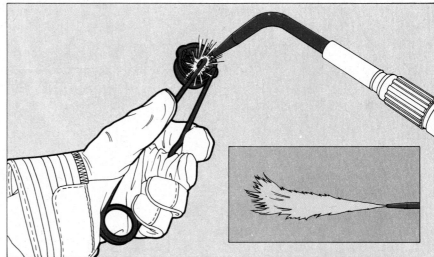

1 **Lighting the torch.** With all valves closed, screw a tip that fits a No. 63 drill onto the torch. Slowly open the acetylene cylinder valve a half turn, open the oxygen cylinder valve completely, then open the regulators by turning the adjusting screws clockwise until each working-pressure gauge registers 5 psi. Hold the round end of a sparklighter about 1 inch from the welding tip, open the acetylene needle valve a quarter turn and snap the handles of the sparklighter together to ignite the gas. Open the acetylene needle valve slowly until the flame becomes somewhat turbulent and stops smoking (inset), then open the oxygen needle valve to produce the neutral flame shown on page 56, top left. Readjust the regulators to reset the working-pressure gauges at 5 psi; make final adjustments at the needle valves to restore the neutral flame. Caution: never lay down a burning torch.

To shut off the torch briefly, close the acetylene needle valve, then the oxygen needle valve. If you are going to leave the welding rig unattended, close both cylinder valves, reopen the needle valves, make sure the regulators are open and wait until the gauges of each regulator read zero; then close the needle valves and turn the regulator adjusting screws counterclockwise to close the regulators.

2 **Carrying a puddle.** Rest a scrap of ⅛-inch steel about 5 inches square between two firebricks and, gripping the torch like a pencil, with the flame at a 55° angle to the steel plate, hold the white inner cone of the flame about ⅛ inch from the steel until a glossy puddle of molten metal forms. Begin moving the flame in circles about ⅜ inch wide, making one circle about every 2 seconds and keeping the cone of flame within the molten area. Edge the flame gradually forward in overlapping ovals as the puddle develops, until you can carry the puddle about 4 inches across the plate, leaving a straight, even trail of ripples (*inset, top*).

If the puddle sags deeply, lessen the angle between the flame and the plate. If the puddle is too small (*inset, middle*), move the flame more slowly. If the puddle grows too large (*inset, bottom*), move the torch forward faster.

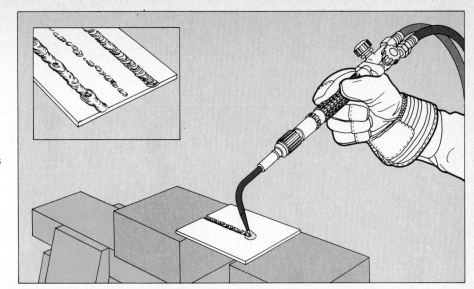

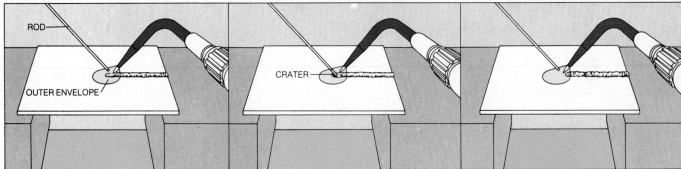

3 **Filling a puddle.** Holding a ³/₃₂-inch filler rod in one hand and the torch in the other, heat the end of the rod in the blue outer envelope of the flame. Start a puddle with the torch (*Step 2*), holding the rod at a 45° angle to the steel plate, about ⅛ inch above the plate and ⅜ inch from the white inner cone of the flame (*left*). As the center of the puddle begins to form a crater, dip the tip of the rod into it (*center*);

continue moving the torch steadily so that the puddle, rather than the flame, melts the rod. When the puddle rises to a slight crown above the plate, pull the rod away and edge the torch forward (*right*). Continue lowering and raising the rod as the puddle forms craters. Practice until you can make a "weld bead" that is about 4 inches long, and has an even, slightly crowned series of ripples.

If metal drips from the rod, hold the rod farther from the puddle and the inner cone of the flame. If the rod sticks to the plate, free it by aiming the torch directly at it; then be sure to dip the rod at the center of the puddle. If the puddle grows too large, move the torch forward faster. If the metal from the rod sticks on the surface of the plate rather than fusing with it, move the torch forward more slowly.

The Two Basic Joints

1 **Welding a butt joint.** For this joint, used to attach ornaments to a grille, rest two pieces of ⅛-inch steel about ¹/₁₆ inch apart between two firebricks. Near each end and at the center, tack-weld the pieces by melting them until the metal flows together (*Step 2*) and building up the joint with filler rod (*Step 3*). Then move the torch and rod along the joint, melting the edges together and reinforcing with filler rod.

Turn the plates over with pliers to see whether the weld penetrated to the bottom of the joint. If the molten metal has dripped (*inset, middle*) you moved the torch too slowly; if the bead does not reach the bottom of the joint (*inset, bottom*), you moved the torch too fast.

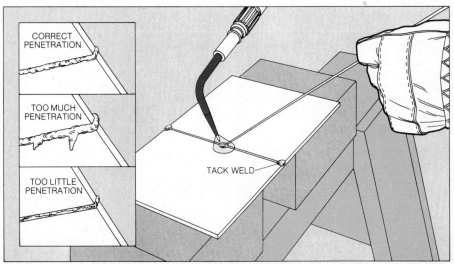

2 Welding a T joint. For this joint, used to attach bars into a grille frame, rest a piece of ⅛-inch steel between two firebricks, hold another piece vertically on top of it with pliers, and tack-weld each end of the joint without using a filler rod *(left)*. Hold the torch overhand, with the tip at a 45° angle to each plate and to the line of the joint, and melt the pieces together into a small puddle; keep the white inner cone as close as possible to the joint but do not allow it to touch the metal. Make sure the heat of the flame is evenly divided between the two pieces.

Make a third tack weld at the center of the joint and reinforce it with ⅛-inch filler rod, holding the rod at a 20° angle to the vertical plate and a 30° angle to the line of the weld. Finally, make a continuous weld along the joint, adding filler rod on the vertical plate *(right)*. Test the weld by clamping one of the pieces in a vise and hammer-ing the other over; the weld should not crack. The weld bead should fill the corner between the vertical and horizontal pieces and penetrate to the "root" of the joint—the line where the two pieces meet. If it does not, make smaller circles with the torch and wait until the puddles are completely molten before adding filler rod. If the vertical plate just above the joint is thin and melted, move the puddle faster and aim the flame more toward the horizontal plate.

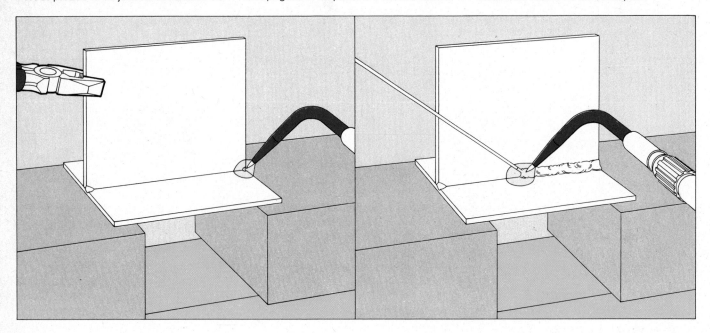

The Torch as a Cutting Tool

Anatomy of a cutting torch. On this typical welding rig, a cutting attachment screws onto the torch body; other rigs have a complete cutting torch that connects to the supply hoses. In either type, an oxygen-acetylene flame from holes around the rim of the cutting tip preheats the steel to about 1,800° F.; then a high-pressure cutting jet of pure oxygen from the larger hole at the center of the tip oxidizes the steel in a shower of sparks and slag. A lever on the back of the torch turns the jet on. The oxygen of the preheat flame is controlled by the needle valve at the base of the lever; the acetylene, by the valve at the base of the torch. The ordinary torch oxygen valve is left wide open.

To prepare the rig to cut ½-inch steel, use a cutting tip with a center hole that fits a No. 62 drill and adjust the acetylene regulator to 5 psi, the oxygen regulator to 25 psi. Light and adjust the flame, then depress the cutting lever. With the lever down, adjust the regulators to restore the correct working pressures and adjust the needle valves for a neutral cutting flame *(page 56, top right)*. Release the lever.

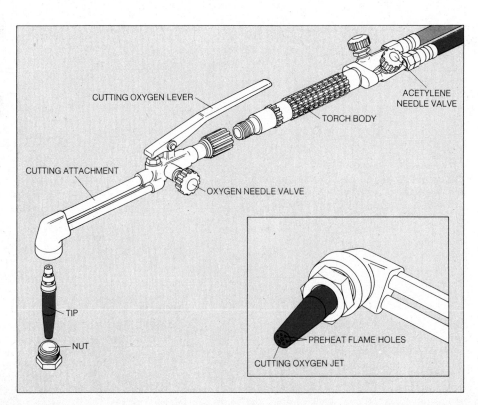

Making a cut. To practice cutting, draw a line across a piece of ½-inch steel plate, ¾ inch from one end, and set the plate on firebricks with the line overhanging the bricks. Holding the torch overhand, with the thumb of one hand on the cutting-oxygen lever and the other hand guiding the torch, position the torch so that the white cone of the preheat flame is ⅛ inch above the line at one edge of the plate.

When the steel beneath the flame becomes bright red (after about 20 seconds), gradually press the cutting-oxygen lever; then, as a cut opens in the plate and sparks and slag begin to shoot down beneath the plate, move the tip slowly along the line at about 1 inch every three seconds (*inset*). Caution: keep your body away from the underside of the plate.

If the cut will not start, preheat the plate for a longer period. If the cut stops, preheat the steel and start the cut again, moving the torch more slowly. If the edges of the cut are ragged, take special care to move the torch in a perfectly straight line. If the top edge of the cut is rounded and melted, move the torch faster.

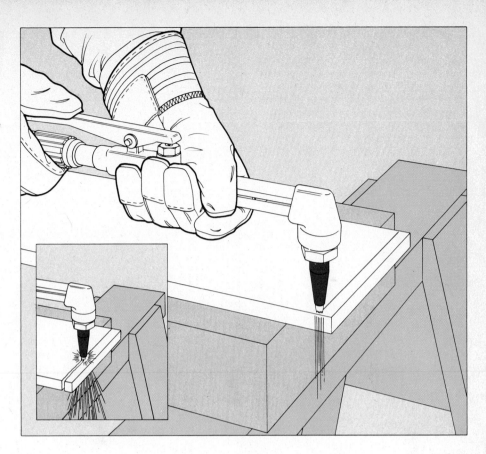

Assembling the Parts

1 Making the jig. To hide the welds, assemble the grille upside down in a homemade jig. Drill ⅝-inch holes, spaced for the pickets, in a 2-by-4; nail it to a slightly shorter 2-by-4 and then between two sawhorses. Hammer the pickets—square ½-inch steel bars the height of the window—into the drilled holes.

Set two firebricks on edge between two pairs of pickets. Slide a spreader—a 1-inch steel channel as long as the width of the grille, with square ½-inch picket holes punched by the supplier—over the pickets, channel side up, and clamp the spreader to the 2-by-4s.

Fasten two 2-by-4s together loosely with carriage bolts and slide this homemade clamp down around the pickets. Set two firebricks on the clamp, then slide another spreader over the pickets, channel side up, and rest it on the firebricks. Have a helper raise the assembly of 2-by-4 clamp, firebricks and bottom spreader, and tighten the 2-by-4 clamp when the spreader is level in its planned location—generally at the same distance from the ends of the pickets as the top one. Secure the spreader to the 2-by-4 clamp with clamps. Check the angles of the pickets and spreaders with a framing square.

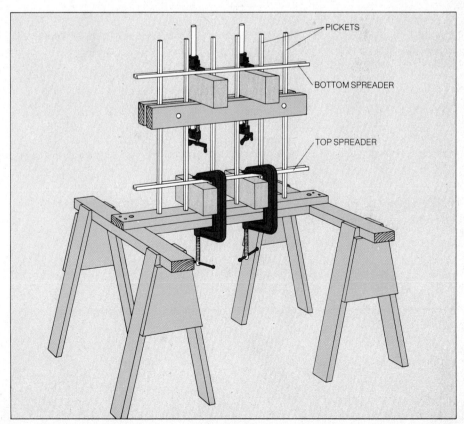

PICKETS

BOTTOM SPREADER

TOP SPREADER

2 **Welding spreaders to pickets.** Set the oxygen working pressure at 5 psi and the acetylene at 5 psi, and use a No. 44-drill welding tip and a ³/₃₂-inch filler rod to weld both sides of each picket to the channel of the bottom spreader, working from the center picket out to each end of the spreader. Hold the torch at a 30° angle to the spreader, with most of the heat aimed at the picket; heat the picket about ¾ inch above the spreader, then aim the flame at the joint and make the actual weld quickly to avoid warping the spreader. Remove the clamps and firebricks, then weld the pickets to the channel of the top spreader in the same way.

If the grille will be bolted inside a window recess (*page 66*), hold narrow, predrilled mounting clips (available from ornamental-iron suppliers) to the top of each channel with pliers, flush with the ends of the channels, and weld them in place (*left inset*). If the grille will be bolted to the face of a wall, weld a 3-inch piece of solid 1-by-½-inch steel bar, called a return, to the end of each spreader and weld wider, ornamental clips to the returns (*right inset*).

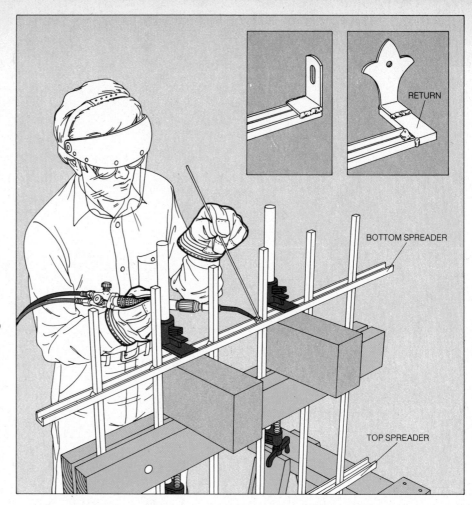

RETURN

BOTTOM SPREADER

TOP SPREADER

Shaping Steel into Ornaments

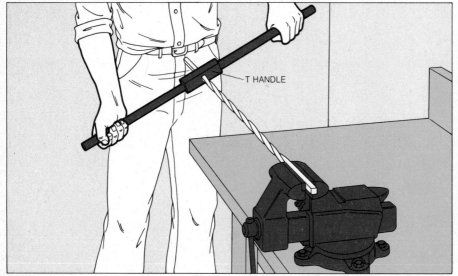

T HANDLE

Twisting a picket. Using a picket as long as the height of the grille, clamp 6 inches of one end into a heavy-duty bench vise and slide a T handle with a square, ½-inch hole—available from steel suppliers—onto the picket and position it

at a point 6 inches from the other end. Rotate the T handle, keeping the handle always parallel to the sides of the vise and counting the number of turns, until the picket has the amount of twist you want and the ends line up squarely.

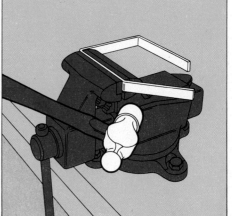

Making a diamond to fit between pickets. For a decorative diamond with equal sides, clamp a ⅛-by-½-inch steel bar in a vise. Bend the bar to a rough 90° angle by hand, then strike the bend with a ball-peen hammer until the corner is perfectly square. Bend the other sides of the diamond in the same way and cut off the extra length of bar. Clamp the diamond closed and weld the ends together on the outer side of the joint.

Bending scrolls and circles. For an S scroll, draw onto ¾-inch plywood a curve like the one at right, with the help of the draftsman's instrument called a French curve, making the notch ¼ inch wide. Cut out the curve, glue and nail it to a larger piece of plywood and nail the assembly to a workbench. Bend one end of a ⅛-by-½-inch steel bar in a vise (*opposite, bottom right*) to fit the notch, slide it into the jig and bend the bar around the curve to make the upper part of the S, then bend the other end of the bar around the jig to complete the S.

To make a plywood jig for a circle, use a compass to draw a circle ¼ inch smaller in diameter than the circle you want. Cut the circle out with a saber saw, nail it to another piece of plywood and nail a small block of wood ⅛ inch from the circle. Slide the end of a ⅛-inch steel bar between the circle and the block and bend the bar around the jig. Cut off the excess, clamp the circle closed and weld the ends together.

NOTCH

Fancy Frills for Bars and Grilles

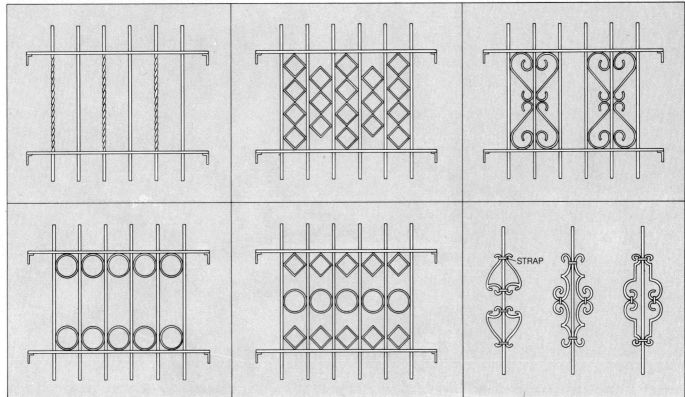

STRAP

A choice of welded patterns. The grilles above vary in the complexity of their designs and welding procedures. In the simplest, at top left, twisted pickets alternate with straight ones, relieving the monotony of a plain grille. In the next four examples, ornaments are welded to the grille and to each other with butt joints on each side of the grille. At top center, offset diamonds create an unobtrusive visual screen for privacy. The rows of circles at bottom left can be used to echo the curves of rounded architectural features, while the mixture of diamonds and circles at bottom center fits better with the angular lines of contemporary architecture. The scrolls at top right, a more traditional motif, strengthen the grille with diagonal bracing. The drawing at bottom right shows three of the many prefabricated ornaments available from ornamental-iron dealers. The stirrup-like straps of these ornaments fit over a picket; the front of the strap and the back of the ornament are welded to the picket.

Sturdy Mountings for a Window

In any grille, the fastening to the window frame is the weakest point, vulnerable to a pry bar or cold chisel. For maximum protection, the ironwork should be mounted inside the house, where the fasteners can reach through the window jamb into a stud. This location, however, prevents the easy operation of the window sash, and grilles in most cases are installed outside.

Custom-made grilles can be screwed to studs through the face of the wall or of the exterior trim, called brickmold. This is not possible with the ready-made type, which must be screwed to the sides of the window frame. In many modern frame homes the outside window recess is so shallow that the only attachment available is the brickmold, generally only ¾ inch thick—not nearly thick enough to hold long screws. A grille installed in this way can deter an intruder but may not foil a determined burglar. In older homes, where the window is recessed more than 2 inches from the outer face of the wall, such grilles can be screwed through the jamb into a stud.

In walls of solid masonry, use expansion anchors (opposite) to secure the screws. The holding power of the anchors depends on the composition of the wall—concrete is strongest, brick weakest—and on the tightness of pilot holes. In old, powdery masonry the bit size recommended by the anchor manufacturer may make too large a hole; experiment with smaller bits until you find one that bores a close-fitting hole.

To bore a pilot hole in solid concrete, you will need a rented hammer-drill and a carbide bit; if the wall is reinforced with steel bars, choose a fastener that can be set into a shallow hole. For a brick wall, use an ordinary drill with a masonry bit and locate the anchors deep in horizontal mortar joints—do not use the weaker vertical joints or the middle of a brick. The outside diameter of the anchor should match the thickness of the mortar joints between bricks (usually ⅜ inch). Avoid the type of anchor that is expanded by a hammer blow—the impact often crumbles the surrounding masonry.

When using any anchor, make sure the length and thread of the screw match those of the anchor. Stop tightening the fastener as soon as you begin to feel substantial resistance; overtightening can cause the anchor to pull out entirely.

To prevent a burglar from removing the fasteners that hold a grille, use screws with one-way heads, available in all sizes of machine and wood screws up to No. 14. If you cannot obtain nonremovable screws or must use larger fasteners—lag bolts, machine bolts or machine nuts—alter the heads with a grinder (page 38).

Using Ready-made Bars

Mounting an adjustable grille in wood. If you must fasten the grille to the brickmolds, telescope the grille against them, center it vertically and have a helper mark the inner edges of the brickmold through the holes in the mounting strips. Drill pilot holes at the marks (page 21, Step 1) and fasten the grille with No. 12 wood screws 1¼ inches long. If you can fasten the grille through the window jamb into the studs, place it against the strip of wood (called a blind spot) next to the window sash, and fasten it with ¼-inch lag bolts 2½ inches long.

BRICKMOLD

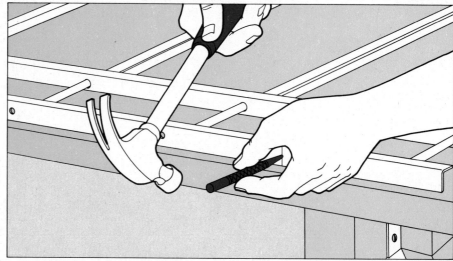

Mounting an adjustable grille in masonry. Center the grille in the opening and mark the mounting strap at intervals of about 8 inches, setting the marks at mortar joints in a brick wall or at the centers of blocks in a masonry-block wall; remove the grille and strike the strap with a center punch opposite each mark. Choose anchors appropriate to the wall (opposite) and drill holes in the strap for the fasteners. Replace the grille, mark each hole's location on the masonry and drill holes for the anchors, then insert the anchors and fasten the grille to them.

Anchors for Masonry Walls

A jute-fiber shield. As a wood screw is tightened, it forces the sides of the shield out against the masonry. This type of screw shield has great holding power but is limited to indoor applications; outdoors, it will eventually rot.

Threaded stud anchors. Designed for use with a machine nut and a washer, these anchors get their strength from especially deep pilot holes. The anchor at top tightens against the masonry when the nut forces a split sleeve over the mushroom-shaped end of the bolt. A few hammer blows tighten the anchor at bottom against the masonry by forcing the tapered pin into the split section of the shank; once tightened, the anchor cannot be removed.

A calking anchor. Especially suitable for shallow holes, this anchor is set with a hammer and a special calking tool provided by the manufacturer. As the tool drives the lead sleeve down over the plug, the bottom of the plug forces the sleeve out against the masonry.

A drop-in anchor. This anchor, suited to old or weak brick walls, is simply inserted into a snug pilot hole. As a machine screw or machine bolt is tightened, wedges at the ends of the anchor force the two sleeves apart, creating an even pressure along the entire length of the hole.

Anchors for concrete blocks. As the hollow-wall anchor at top is tightened, the four leaves of the metal sleeve fold and expand against the inside of the block to lock the sleeve in place. The toggle bolt shown at bottom provides excellent holding power in weak materials such as crumbly cinder block; the toggle unfolds in the space inside a block and is pulled back against the wall of the block as the bolt is tightened.

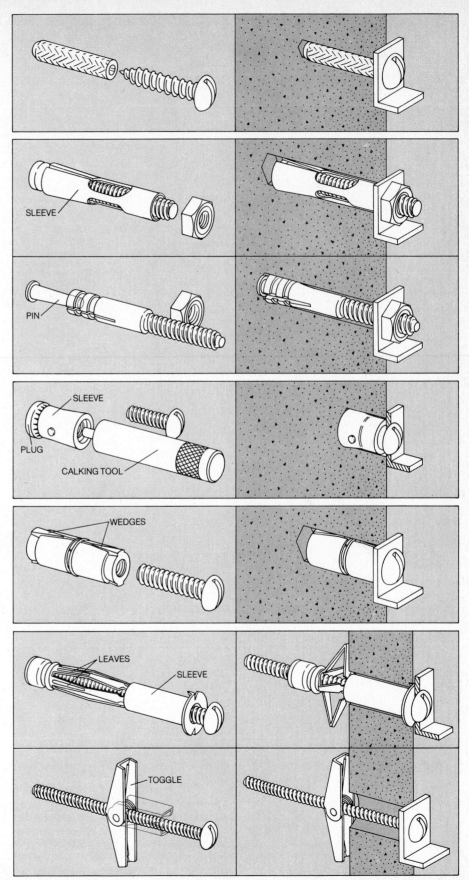

A clanging in the night. Fastened to a panel inside a weather-tight box, an outdoor burglar-alarm bell can be mated with a flashing light (*page 92*) mounted on the cover of the box to pinpoint a house where a burglar has attempted a break-in. The bell and light, like the rest of a central system, operate on low voltage, making bulky wires unnecessary and simplifying the routing of wires through the house.

Electric alarm systems are more than a century old. Indeed, they predate the telephone, and Thomas Watson, Alexander Graham Bell's assistant in the invention of that ubiquitous instrument, acquired much of his considerable electrician's skill by installing alarms during the 1860s. One of the earliest alarm systems in the United States was patented in 1853 by Alexander Pope of Boston. Simpler than, but surprisingly similar to, modern electronic devices, Pope's invention consisted of pairs of electromagnetic contacts mounted at doors and windows and connected with copper wire to a battery and a bell. When a window or door was disturbed and the contacts were separated, the bell rang. The chief drawback—the network could be easily defeated by cutting the wire—has been remedied in the best of today's alarm systems.

Those early devices, as well as later ones for detecting fire, were installed in business buildings and in homes of the wealthy by protection services that also monitored the system for alarms. The same security can be purchased today, although it is expensive. Far less costly are alarms that you can install yourself to detect intruders, fire and, in sophisticated systems, a wide variety of other dangers.

The simplest of burglar alarms are not fundamentally different from Alexander Pope's invention. They employ a contact for the door or window and use a battery to sound a buzzer. But unlike Pope's device, these alarms are self-contained, with battery, buzzer, wiring and, in most types, contact for window or door all in one box. There are self-contained alarms for fire as well as for burglary and neither type requires more than a few screws to install (*pages 70-73*). Yet there are limitations to these one-piece alarms. They sound off loudly when they are disturbed, but perhaps not loudly enough to frighten away a determined burglar—who, in any case, can silence almost any of them by merely closing the door or window he has forced open or, if he knows how the device works, by reaching through the opening to switch off the alarm.

Central alarm systems suffer from neither of these faults. When a burglar opens a door or window fitted with contacts, the control box that serves as the brain of the system instantly activates a clangorous bell (*opposite*) that can arouse an entire neighborhood; the bell cannot be silenced unless the burglar finds the box where it is concealed. In many such systems, tampering with the alarm box beforehand—or cutting any of the wires in the system—will set off the alarm instead of deactivating the system. And most central alarm systems have been designed to be connected to sensors that will alert your family to almost any danger, from a smashed window to a smouldering fire or a flooded basement.

69

A Warning System Complete in a Screw-on Box

Smoke from a smouldering living-room sofa curls toward the bedroom hallway while you and your family are asleep. Suddenly, an alarm blares from an inconspicuous box on the hallway ceiling and, roused from sleep, everyone leaves the house quickly—and safely.

A stranger approaches your home while you are away. Slipping to the side of the house, he starts to raise an unlocked window. A piercing alarm sounds out, and the would-be intruder hurries away from a home that is protected against burglary by an intrusion alarm.

Providing your home with such protection against fire and intrusion need not require an expensive, centrally controlled security system and a maze of wires. Easily mounted, self-contained smoke detectors *(page 73)* give ample warning of a fire and, in a relatively low-crime area, inexpensive intrusion alarms like the ones on these pages are adequate. None of them call for electrical wiring.

The most common intrusion alarm is a battery-operated spot protector. Set on a door or window, it buzzes loudly when the door or window is opened. The models shown here can be bought at hardware and electronic-equipment stores, and are especially useful for a limited number of entrance points.

A simple spot protector *(below)* can be set to sound an alarm only while you are inside the house. It makes enough noise to alert you and to frighten off most potential intruders, but an intruder who stays long enough to see where the noise is coming from can silence the alarm by simply flicking the ON/OFF switch. The more costly model at the top of the opposite page, which is set with a removable key, is more difficult to silence. It comes with a special disarming switch in addition to the ON/OFF switch, and lets you turn the protector on, then come and go without tripping the alarm.

More sophisticated than any spot protector is an ultrasonic space alarm *(page 72)*, which plugs into an electrical outlet. This alarm fills a "trap zone" inside the home with high-frequency sound waves, inaudible to the human ear; the alarm is triggered when the wave pattern is disturbed by any motion. Aimed across the areas an intruder must cross, a single unit can protect an entire house.

Ultrasonic alarms have their disadvantages. Drafts and vibrations can cause false alarms, and an intruder who spots the unit can easily turn it off. But the false-alarm problem can be lessened by careful placement *(page 72, bottom),* and a remote speaker in another room will keep an intruder from following the sound of the alarm directly to the unit.

Spot Protection for Doors and Windows

A door-chain alarm. Mount the battery-powered alarm unit at the edge of the door about 18 inches above the doorknob, and position the chain bracket on the doorframe to allow about ½ inch of slack in the chain when the door is closed and the chain knob is at the center of the alarm slot. When the unit is on and the door is opened, the chain is pulled taut and its knob moves from the center to the side of the slot. There, it presses two electrical contacts together, so that the electrical circuit of the alarm is activated and the buzzer sounds.

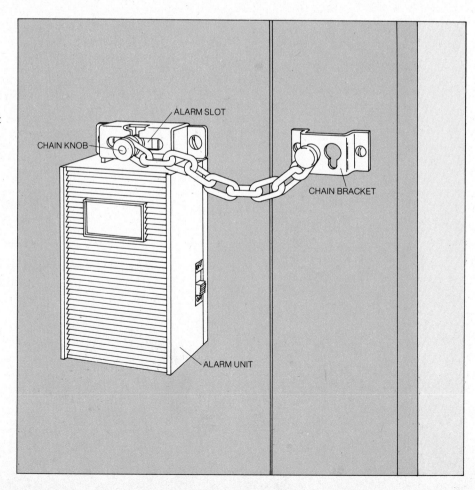

ALARM SLOT

CHAIN KNOB

CHAIN BRACKET

ALARM UNIT

A locking door alarm. Mount the alarm unit about ⅛ inch from the door edge and 18 inches above the knob; mount the sensor at the edge of the doorframe, ¼ inch below the top of the unit. The battery-powered alarm sounds when contact between two magnetic sensors—one in the alarm unit and one on the doorframe—is broken.

Because the alarm is set with a key, an intruder cannot silence the buzzer by switching it off. With the disarming switch at the IN position, the buzzer will sound as soon as the door is opened, and will continue to sound until turned off with the key; closing the door will not stop the sound. With the switch at OUT, there is a delay of 30 seconds before the alarm sounds, giving an occupant time to leave and enter the house without sounding the buzzer. An indicator light glows when the unit is activated, and a cutoff button keeps the alarm from sounding when the door is opened from inside.

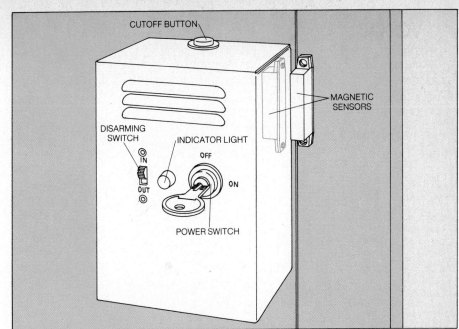

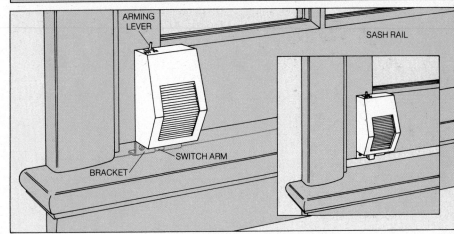

A window buzzer. Fasten this battery-powered unit to the bottom rail of a window sash by pushing the prongs of its bracket up into the bottom of the rail and sticking it in place, using its adhesive backing strip. Set the arming lever to ON. With the window closed, a spring-loaded switch arm is retracted by the pressure of the window sill; if an intruder raises the window (inset), the switch arm is released to complete the electrical circuit and sound the alarm.

The Ultimate Alarm—A Family Dog

Perhaps the most reliable security system is a living one—the family dog. Self-contained, requiring neither electricity nor installation, it can be trained to respond to most dangers or threats of danger. Almost any dog will raise an alarm in response to intrusion or fire, but differences in temperament make some better watchdogs than others.

When choosing a puppy as a combination pet and alarm, test its behavior. Puppies that come when called, follow readily with their tails down and submit to handling after only a brief struggle will generally fit into nearly any household, including one with small children.

Puppies that come and follow with their tails up, nipping at your hands or heels and struggling and biting when handled have more aggressive temperaments. With patience and training they make fine pets, but nipping can remain a problem. Puppies that will not come or follow at all, and that do not struggle when handled, may be too independent to be easily trained.

Once you have taken it home, a puppy will need only obedience training and loving care to develop the combination of aggressive and submissive qualities that make a good family watchdog. You can train a dog yourself at obedience classes offered in many areas or with the help of one of the many books available on the subject.

Further protection training is unnecessary for family pets. Dogs that go beyond the sounding of an alarm to attack intruders are not recommended as family pets, although some people living alone prefer aggressive "one-man" dogs. A dog trained to bite any hand that holds a weapon or attack any suspicious person is generally advisable only to protect commercial property.

Patrolling with Silent Sound

An ultrasonic motion detector. High-frequency sound waves fan outward in an elongated oval from the front of this compact unit, which is powered by 120-volt house current. The waves are reflected from objects in the protected area and the detector compares the pitch of the echoes with that of the original waves. When no movement occurs the pitches are identical; any motion causes a discrepancy, and the alarm sounds. The unit's speaker can be set to sound a loud, hornlike alarm; an indicator light behind the grille glows when the alarm is triggered.

All controls are located at the rear of the unit (*below, right*). A power switch turns the unit on and off—a 20-to-30-second delay feature permits you to activate the unit and leave the room without tripping the alarm. An electrical outlet is provided to plug in a lamp, which then will light automatically when the alarm is triggered, startling a nighttime intruder with sudden light as well as sound.

A speaker switch turns the alarm horn on and off; with the switch in the OFF position, the indicator light can be used to test the unit without sounding

the horn. Delay switches for the alarm and the lamp outlet set horn and lamp for activation either at the instant a motion is detected or after a 20-second delay; this feature allows you to enter the protected area while the alarm is on, and shut it off before it sounds.

The alarm-time switch determines how long the alarm will sound each time it is set off. On most units the coverage area can be set to extend about 8 feet from the face of the unit, about 15 feet, or about 24 feet.

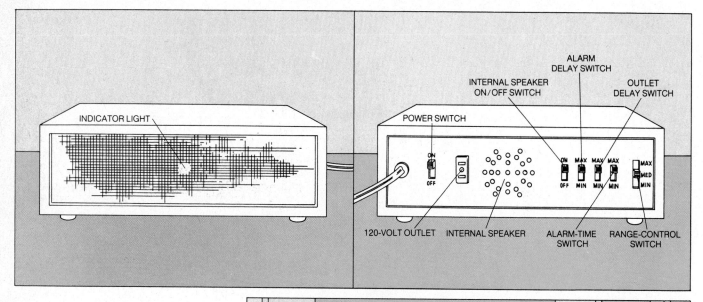

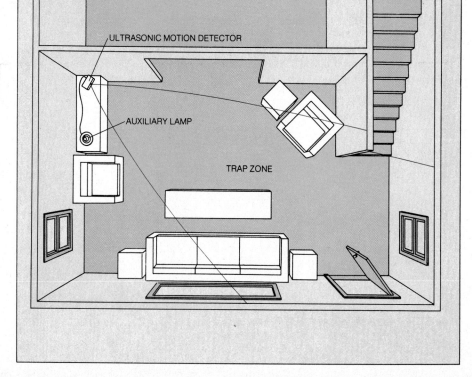

Positioning an ultrasonic detector. Place the unit so that its pattern of sound waves covers entrances and exits, and so that an intruder could not move from the protected room to any other part of the house without tripping the alarm. To prevent false alarms, do not aim the pattern at a 90° angle toward such vibrating surfaces as doors and windows, or toward such sources of drafts as stairways.

Where to Put Smoke Detectors

Smaller than a cigar box and easily fastened to any ceiling or wall, a smoke detector is the least expensive form of fire protection you can buy. Placed correctly, it sounds a warning early enough to enable you to escape from even a major fire. There are two basic types, ionization and photoelectric.

In an ionization chamber, bits of harmless radioactive material flood the gap between two terminals with a cloud of electrically conductive atomic particles. Normally an electrical current is carried between the terminals by the particles, but the smoke from a fire reduces the flow of current and triggers the alarm. In a photoelectric detector, the alarm is tripped when smoke in the chamber deflects a beam of light onto a switch sensitive to light.

Ionization detectors respond quickly to smoke from clean-burning fires of paper and wood. However, they tend to sound false alarms when exposed to normal household fumes and kitchen smoke. Photoelectric detectors respond slowly to clean-burning fires, but quickly to the slow-burning, smouldering fires that occur most frequently in homes—that produce heavy smoke and are most likely to start in a kitchen, basement, bedroom, living room or den.

The placement of a smoke detector is critical. Since most fatal fires occur at night, detectors should be installed in hallways near bedrooms. Some smoke detectors also contain heat sensors, which are useful in furnace rooms, where a rapid rise in temperature can occur before fire breaks out. Detectors in still other parts of the home (right, above) provide additional protection.

Although some detectors operate on house current, battery-powered models have no wires and are easy to install wherever you need them. They also continue to provide protection in the event of a power failure. Most detectors sound a beep when the battery runs low. Generally, batteries need to be changed about once a year.

Smoke detectors should be tested once a month. Most photoelectric models have a test button that simulates smoke by passing a thin wire through the beam of light in the detector chamber; ionization detectors are generally tested by blowing smoke through the unit. An occasional cleaning prevents dust build-ups that can cause a detector to malfunction or to sound false alarms.

Locating detectors in a house. Install at least one detector on every floor of a house. Set one at the head of a stairwell, and protect sleeping areas with a detector in an adjoining hallway; smokers should install one in the bedroom. Place additional detectors in rooms where fires commonly start, such as living rooms and kitchens; in a kitchen, use a photoelectric model, which will not react to normal cooking fumes.

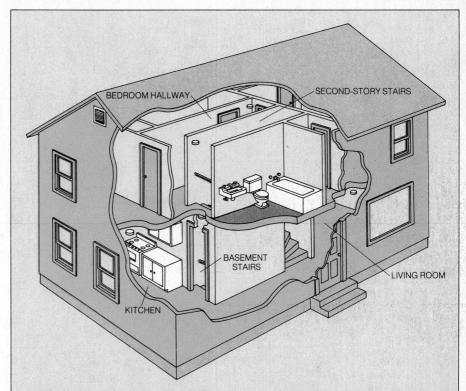

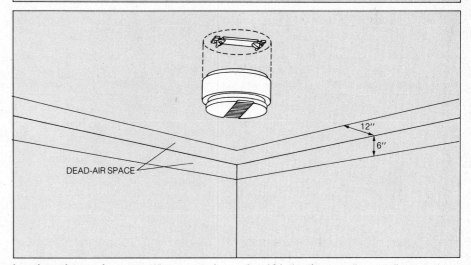

Locating a detector in a room. Wherever possible, place a smoke detector at the center of the ceiling. If this location is not practical, follow these guidelines to avoid dead air spaces, in which the smoke from a fire is unlikely to circulate and a detector will be useless. In most rooms, avoid installing a ceiling-mounted detector less than 12 inches from a wall, or a wall-mounted unit less than 6 inches from the ceiling. In rooms that have a cathedral or A-frame ceiling, position the smoke detector about 12 inches below the peak of the ceiling. On a beamed ceiling, install the detector on the bottom of a beam, not in the space between beams.

A Network of Protection from a Central System

Burglary and fire protection for more than a room or two is best provided by a central system consisting of alarms and sensors linked to a control box by inexpensive, light-gauge wire. Such a system is more versatile and easier to maintain than a collection of single-room alarms because it employs only one control box, and that box can handle all the types of sensing devices needed to protect the whole house. A central system also is harder for an intruder to defeat because the alarms are located well away from the sensors, and thus are not easy for him to track down and silence.

The brain of a central system is the control box, which continuously monitors the network of heat, smoke and intrusion sensors mounted throughout the house. Should any sensor trip, the message is relayed through the box to signaling devices, audible or visible alarms. The control box should have circuits for at least two kinds of alarms, one for fire and another for intrusion. Additional warning devices for each type can then be added to each circuit to provide an outside bell, horn or flashing light to alert neighbors as well as inside alarms to alert occupants of the house. Power for the system comes from batteries, house current or a combination of the two *(page 99)*.

Simple control boxes are generally available at electrical-supply stores, hardware stores and department stores. For more sophisticated ones you will have to consult local distributors of alarm equipment, listed in the classified telephone directory under Burglar Alarm Systems. Buy sensors, switches and battery or transformer where you get the control box in order to be certain that all the parts will work together.

The control box can be mounted in any out-of-the-way location; most people choose a basement wall or the back of a closet. Connections to alarms and sensors are made with insulated 18-gauge copper wire meant for 6- or 12-volt current. Because of the low voltages involved, electrical-code regulations that restrict 120-volt wiring do not apply. The wires can be snaked from component to component behind walls, hidden behind baseboards or even stapled in the open along walls or joists *(pages 78-82)*.

The numbers and types of sensors you need depend on the size and layout of your house. Fire sensors should be located in the same way as single-unit smoke detectors *(page 73)*. Intrusion sensors—magnetic, mercury or push-button switches, or strips of metallic window tape—are needed for each first-floor window and door. Intrusion sensors should also be installed on any second-floor window that is easily reached—from a porch or a climbable tree, for example. Wherever doors or windows are hidden in the back of the house or by shrubbery, providing concealment for a skillful burglar to disarm the sensor, you may want to add heat-sensitive, infrared, ultrasonic or pressure-sensitive interior motion detectors, or trip-wire switches *(pages 86-89)* to your system.

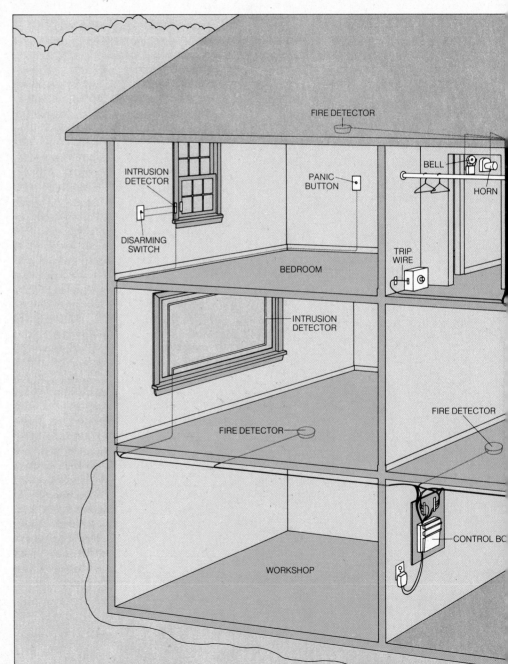

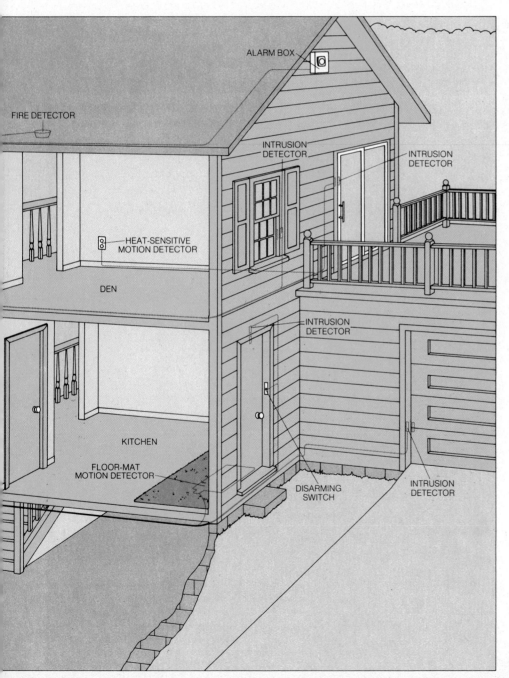

ALARM BOX

FIRE DETECTOR

INTRUSION DETECTOR

INTRUSION DETECTOR

HEAT-SENSITIVE MOTION DETECTOR

DEN

INTRUSION DETECTOR

KITCHEN

FLOOR-MAT MOTION DETECTOR

DISARMING SWITCH

INTRUSION DETECTOR

A central alarm system. In the house at left a control box mounted on the basement wall is connected by wires to an array of strategically located trouble sensors, signals and disarming, or disconnect, switches. Fire sensors are placed in the upstairs hall, in the bedroom, in the basement workshop and above the basement stairs. All accessible windows and doors are fitted with intrusion sensors backed up by motion detectors at the kitchen door and in the upstairs den, and by a trip wire in the upstairs closet.

A disarming switch at the kitchen door allows residents to turn the system on and off as they leave or return; the switch next to the bedroom window disarms only that window so that it can be opened for ventilation. A panic button in the bedroom permits a resident to sound an alarm manually. An inside burglary bell and a loud fire horn are located in the upstairs hall and an alarm box combining a bell and flashing light are located on the outside wall.

How Electronic Alarms Work: Two Basic Circuits

Wired alarm systems are triggered in one of two ways—by making an electrical connection or by breaking one. In the first type, the sensors interrupt the electrical path of the circuit so long as they are not tripped; the circuit is said to be open—no current flows—until an intruder or fire trips a sensor and closes it. Then current passes through the system and triggers the alarm.

Because open circuits can be defeated simply by cutting a wire—so that tripping a sensor does not complete the circuit—they are seldom used to protect the perimeter of the house against intruders. Open circuits are usually used for fire sensors or for floor-mat motion detectors in relatively secure, interior locations.

In the second type of circuit, the electrical path is normally closed at every sensor and a small current flows constantly. When a sensor is tripped it breaks the circuit and a device in the control box reacts to the voltage drop to touch off an alarm. In this system a break in a wire sets off the alarm.

In both kinds of circuits, a device in the control box makes it impossible to silence the signal just by returning the sensor to the untripped position. This safeguard prevents a burglar from turning off the alarm simply by shutting a window or door he has just opened.

Certain types of sensors can be used only in one kind of circuit. And since you cannot mix open and closed sensors on the same circuit, you may need to buy a control box that can operate both kinds of circuit at the same time.

Wiring an open circuit. When more than one sensor is wired into an open circuit, they must be linked together in a pattern called parallel wiring. Each wire from the control box is attached to separate terminals on the first sensor, then runs from those terminals to the corresponding ones on the next sensor. As many sensors as needed can be added in the same way.

The Open Circuit

An open-circuit sensor. The floor-mat sensor contains strips of metal that normally remain apart (*below*), preventing the flow of current. When the mat is stepped on (*bottom*), the conductors are pressed together, letting current flow to the control box to trigger an alarm.

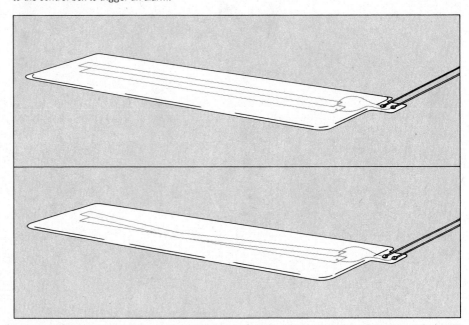

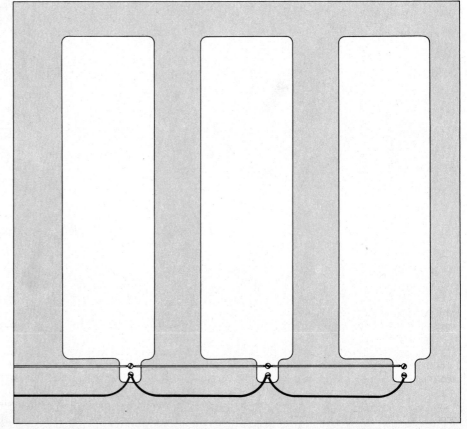

The Closed Circuit

A closed-circuit sensor. In this magnetic window sensor, a magnet mounted on the window sash attracts a metal bar that is concealed inside the switch mounted on the jamb (*left*). The bar holds two electrical contacts tightly closed and allows current to flow continuously through the switch. When the window sash is slid open (*right*), the magnet is carried away from the switch. Because the bar is no longer held in place by the magnet, a tension spring pulls the contacts apart and the flow of current is interrupted, triggering the alarm.

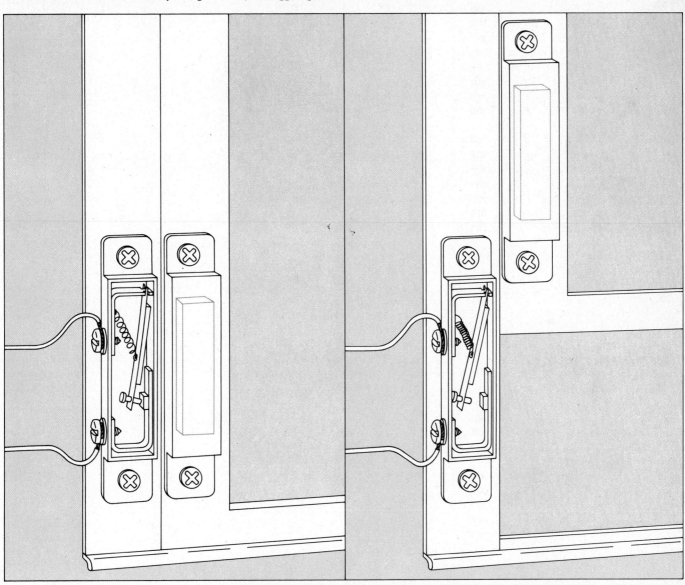

Wiring a closed circuit. When more than one sensor is wired into a closed circuit, the sensors must be linked in a pattern of series wiring. A single wire runs from the control box to one terminal on the first sensor. A second wire links the second terminal on the sensor to the first terminal on the next sensor. The wiring is continued this way up to the last sensor on the circuit; its second terminal is wired to the control box.

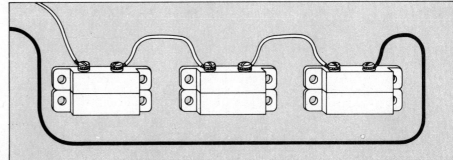

How to Snake Wires through the House

Because there is little danger of shock or fire from the low-voltage wiring used for alarm systems, the cables are light and flexible and they need not be installed according to the rigorous code provisions that govern ordinary house wiring. They can be run anywhere except within 2 inches of house wiring—tucked under carpets, hidden behind moldings or threaded through heating ducts, provided the insulation is fireproof.

The easiest wiring route for an alarm sensor or switch is in an unfinished attic or basement. First run the cable for the circuit through the unfinished room to a location directly above or below a sensor or switch. Use a staple gun with a special slip-on wiring attachment to secure the cables along exposed joists; wherever you cross joists, string the cable through ⅜-inch holes in the joists.

Next, make the short run—typically, less than 4 feet—through the inside of a wall from the unfinished room to the alarm component. For this part of a run either fish a loop of the circuit cable from the basement or attic, or snake a separate lead that later can be connected into the circuit. The tools you will need include two spring-steel fish tapes for pulling wires through walls; a straightened wire coat hanger, which makes a handy tool for poking a path through packed insulation and for fishing a wire or cable over a short distance; and a long electrician's

extension bit for your drill. (You can save some work by using the flexible bit shown at the bottom of the opposite page, which may be worth its cost if you have many sensors to wire.)

In most houses, at least one long vertical run is unavoidable, to get wires from the basement or attic to components on a distant floor. Since every house has at least one plumbing stack running from the basement to the roof, the excess space along this stack (*page 87*) offers an excellent route for alarm wires. Other vertical paths lie inside laundry chutes, heating ducts or unused chimneys, or alongside radiator pipes.

Closets on successive levels of a house also provide a handy vertical path for wiring. If the closets are stacked directly over each other, simply drill up through the ceiling of one into the floor of the next. If they are offset, you may be able to fish wire a short distance through a joist space shared by the closets; alternatively, you can run the wire out of the top of a lower closet to a molding, then into the bottom of an upper closet.

When running wires through closets or unfinished rooms is impossible, look for other ways to avoid long, tricky fishes through walls. Tuck (and staple) wire along the edges of wall-to-wall carpets (a crochet hook to lift the edge of the carpet is sometimes helpful); hide wire behind baseboards, chair rails, picture-

hanging moldings, ceiling moldings or door and window casings. If you hide wires or cables under rugs or carpeting, avoid places where the insulation could be damaged or the wires broken by foot traffic or furniture.

Most sensors require two 18-gauge stranded wires. Use two-conductor cable rather than the less expensive zip cord or lamp cord: the extra layer of sheathing on the cable protects the wires as they are fished around the house. For runs from the control box to the remote-control stations shown on pages 94-96, you will need five-conductor cable; smoke detectors require four-conductor solid-wire cable. In figuring the length of a run, add an extra foot for each connection and buy 20 per cent more than the total estimate, since the wires rarely will run in a straight path. If you need more than 300 feet of any one kind of wire, buy it in an economical 500-foot roll.

To guarantee secure, long-lasting connections, solder them. An inexpensive soldering iron with a 25- to 50-watt heating element will serve, though a soldering gun can speed the job. Whichever tool you choose, sandpaper the pieces to be connected before beginning the job, and be sure to use rosin-core electrical solder; the acid core in plumbing solder weakens electrical connections. Wrap the completed connection tightly with electrician's tape.

Hanging the control box. On the masonry wall of an unfinished basement, use masonry nails to mount a piece of ¾-inch plywood large enough for the control box and terminal strips; on a finished wall, nail through the plywood and wallboard into the studs. While a helper levels the control box on the bottom half of the plywood, drive screws through the mounting holes in the back of the box. Screw the two terminal strips to the plywood vertically, about 6 inches above the control box and 6 inches apart.

A Flexible Drill Bit that Goes around Corners

For decades, electricians engaged in the tricky job of pulling new wires through existing walls have probed with fish tapes. In recent years, however, many have turned to a new tool *(right)* that speeds their work. It is a drill bit with a hole in each end, joined to a flexible, spring-steel shaft. This combination makes it possible to drill through walls, then attach wires or cables to the bit and pull them through the hole as the bit is withdrawn. The special bit, available with shaft either 4½ or 6 feet long, is particularly handy for short runs from a door or window alarm sensor to a basement or attic.

For best results, use the flexible bit with a variable-speed reversible drill. First, using a regular bit, drill through the jamb at the sensor location, angling the hole toward the attic or basement as you drill, then switch to the flexible bit to complete the hole. When you feel the bit emerge from the studs of the rough frame, stop the drill and slide the bit forward until it strikes the next stud, which will deflect it to the plate. Drill through the plate.

To pull the wires back, you will need a special recovery accessory *(inset)*, consisting of a wire basket and a hook

that closes like a safety pin and fastens the basket to the bit through the hole. The link between the hook and its basket is a fish swivel, which permits the drill to run in reverse for the withdrawal of the bit without twisting the wires.

These flexible bits and pulling ac-cessories are available at electrical and alarm-system supply houses. Other helpful accessories for the bit include alignment handles and guide tubes to guide the bit in curves more extreme than the one shown here, and exten-sions for drilling as far as 10 feet.

Wiring from an Unfinished Basement or Attic

1 **Drilling through the plate.** In a room above a basement, bore a small location hole through the floor, just outside the wall space through which you will pull wires, and poke a scrap of stiff wire down through the hole; then, working in the basement, find the wire and drill up through the sole plate of the wall with a long bit. Because there is little room between the plate of an exterior wall and the foundation, you may have to angle the bit to hit the plate; to get inside an interior partition, you can drill straight up.

To run wires down from an attic, follow the same procedure but drill the location hole in the ceiling and drill down from the attic through the top plate of the wall. Adapt the second step of the job (*below*) in the same way.

2 **Fishing the wires.** Drill a hole from the sensor location and push the end of a fish tape through it and behind the wall. Have a helper push a second tape through the hole you have drilled in the plate and maneuver both tapes until their ends catch. In an exterior wall filled with insulation, use the natural curl of the fish tape to keep it between the inside face of the wallboard and the vapor barrier of the insulation.

Pull the hooked tapes into the basement, unhook them, attach the wires to the upper tape and pull it back through the wall.

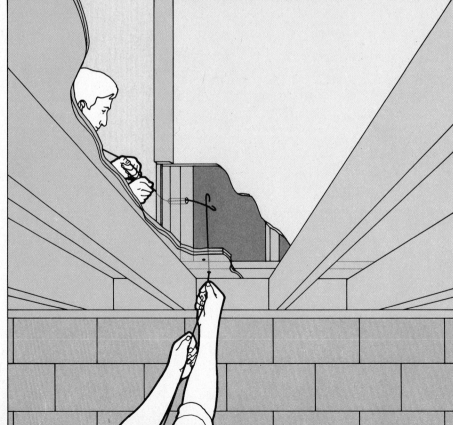

Wiring Up along the Plumbing Stack

Running wires along a stack vent. From the attic, lower a small fishing weight attached to a long piece of heavy string into the excess space alongside the plumbing stack. If the weight is blocked, jiggle and bounce it until it falls past the obstruction. Continue feeding the string until the weight emerges in the basement. Attach the wires to the string, staggering the points of attachment to avoid a bulky connection (*inset*), and have a helper push them up along the stack as you draw the string back to the attic.

Running wires through closets. When closets are not stacked directly above one another, fish wires from the basement through a hole drilled in the floor of a closet above; then drill a hole through the closet ceiling and into the space between the joists above. Drill a hole down into the same joist space through the floor of a closet on the next floor, and feed a length of heavy string, secured to the floor with a nail, into the hole. Push a fish tape toward the string from the lower closet (*inset*). Twist the tape to snag the string, pull it back to the lower closet, tie the string to the wires and pull them into the upper closet. Drill through the ceiling of the upper closet and into the attic. Pull extra wire into each closet and staple it neatly to the wall.

If the closets do not share a joist space, remove a section of baseboard in an upper room and drill behind it on an angle into the joist space above the lower closet. Fish the wires through and run them behind the baseboard (*page 82*) to the nearest closet or sensor.

Running Wire in a Finished Room

Hiding wires behind baseboards. Insert the blade of a wood chisel between the wall and the top of the baseboard and, working from one end of the baseboard to the other, carefully lever it away from the wall. Push the wires into the gap between the floor and the bottom of the wallboard; if there is no gap, cut a groove for the wires along the wall, using a utility knife to cut away wallboard and using a hammer and cold chisel for plaster. Nail the baseboard back in place, angling the nails to avoid the wires.

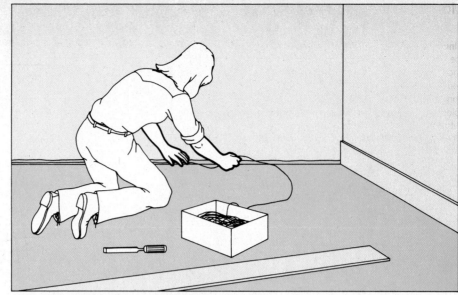

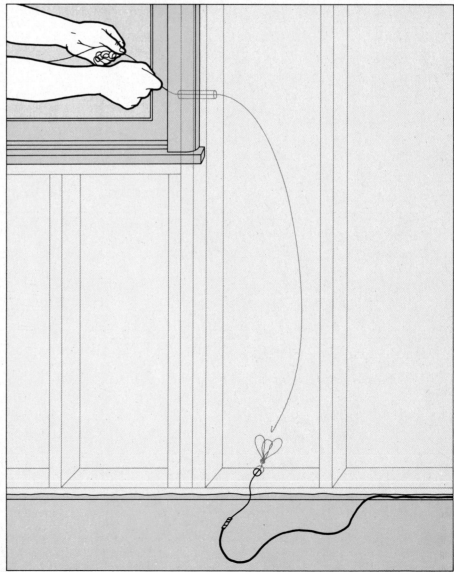

Fishing wires from behind a baseboard. At one end of a piece of springy copper wire, gather three 4-inch loops in a bouquet-like pattern. Attach the alarm cable to the other end of the wire. Directly below the sensor location, drill a hole in the wall behind the baseboard and push the bouquet through it. Push a fish tape toward the bouquet from the sensor hole; when you feel it hit the wire loops, twist it to snag them. Slowly retrieve the tape to pull the bouquet and cable out through the installation hole.

Making Solder Connections

Tinning a lead. Strip ¾ inch of insulation from the lead, twist the strands of wire together tightly and heat the wire with the soldering iron. Touch the solder to the heated wire—not to the iron—and let it flow evenly over the lead. The solder should begin to flow almost instantly; if it does not, remove the solder, heat the wire a little longer and try again.

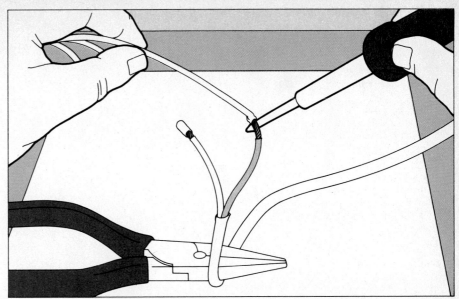

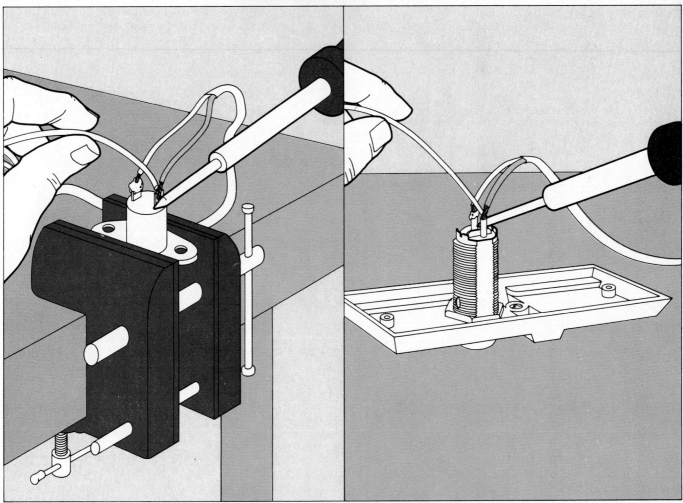

Two basic connections. To connect a wire to a tab connector (*above, left*), pull the tinned end of the wire through the hole in the tab with long-nose pliers and wrap the wire in a loop around the tab. Heat the tab on one side and dab enough solder on the other side to cover the joint smoothly. To secure a lead to a tube connector (*above, right*), insert the tinned lead into the tube, then heat the bottom of the tube until the solder flows into it to grip the wire.

Sensors: The Eyes and Ears that Detect Trouble

A versatile centrally controlled alarm system requires a variety of sensors, detection devices that signal the control box when something is amiss—when a window or door has been opened, or someone is moving around inside the house or smoke has entered a hallway. For each of these dangers and many others, there are several types of sensor.

Most central alarm systems are installed mainly to warn of intruders, and the sooner your system detects them, the better. First protect the "perimeter" with sensors at exterior doors and accessible windows—those less than 8 feet above the ground or next to a porch or balcony. Once the perimeter is secure, you may want additional sensors to detect a burglar who breaches the perimeter and gets inside the house *(page 89)*.

For the perimeter, the most popular sensor is a two-piece magnetic type: a magnetically tripped switch for the frame and a magnet for the door or window *(opposite)*. The magnet holds the switch open or closed—depending on the circuit in which it is installed *(pages 76-77)*; when the door or window is opened, the magnet moves and trips the switch. Also common is a one-piece push button *(right)* that operates on the same principle as a refrigerator-light switch.

Both magnetic and push-button sensors are available in models that can be recessed for concealment or, more simply, screwed to structural surfaces. The surface-mounted type is generally used for metal windows, in which the large hole required for a recessed sensor is impractical to drill. A special wide-gap sensor is available for such applications as a garage door, where the switch and magnet may be spaced more than the standard ¼ to ¾ inch apart.

On double-hung windows and sliding windows and doors, you can install surface-mounted magnetic sensors in such a way *(opposite, bottom right)* that you can open the window or door a few inches for ventilation without tripping the alarm. For doors and casement windows, attach magnetic sensors near the unhinged side, so that the alarm will sound at the slightest opening. After installation, cover exposed terminals by plastering them with epoxy putty.

Although magnetic and push-button sensors are the varieties most commonly used for perimeter protection, other types are used in special situations. An inexpensive wire trap can guard windows or doors, either rigged as a trip wire or set to detect a burglar who enters the house by removing an air conditioner from a window *(page 86)*. For an awning window, a mercury sensor *(pages 86-87)*—which contains a pool of mercury that opens or closes the alarm circuit when tilted—can be adjusted to allow the window to open a few inches before the alarm will sound.

Picture windows and sliding glass doors, which permit an intruder to walk right through if he smashes or cuts all of the glass, present a special problem. The least expensive and most practical solution is provided by a strip of foil glued around the perimeter of the glass *(pages 87-88)*. The foil tears when the glass is broken and triggers an alarm. The foil is used with simple connector blocks on fixed glazing, such as picture windows, but it is necessary to add spring contacts for sliding doors and windows that open. Unlike most sensors, which are available for either an open or a closed circuit, foil must be wired in closed circuit.

Inside the house, the presence of an intruder can be detected in several ways. A floor-mat sensor emits signals when someone steps on it. Unless you are confident of your carpeting skills, have professionals install floor mats on stairs or under wall-to-wall carpeting. Several types of motion detectors send out beams of undetectable sound waves, radio waves or light waves that sound alarms when their beams are interrupted. These motion detectors, like the infrared sensor on page 89, which sends out rays of invisible light, may be disguised as wall outlets, lamps or hi-fi speakers. They generally require four wire connections—two for the alarm circuit and two for a power supply. Another variety of sensor responds to body heat.

Before installing any sensor—except a mercury switch or foil—test it. Ultrasonic, microwave and infrared sensors include a test light. With simpler sensors, use a continuity tester: when the probes of the tester, which consists of a battery and a light, are touched to the terminals of a sensor for an open circuit, the light should glow. Be sure to keep the magnet of a magnetic sensor several inches from the switch. For a closed circuit, the light should not light. After installing a whole system, test each sensor while a helper stands by at a control station.

Triggers Recessed in Doors and Windows

Installing a push-button sensor. For a door, drill a sensor hole in the hinge side of the jamb, removing weather stripping if necessary. Fish circuit wires *(pages 78-82)* and connect them to sensor terminals, then push the wires into the hole and screw the sensor to the jamb. Recess the sensor's mounting flange into the jamb only if the door fits very tightly. If the door closes without activating the switch, glue a shim to the edge of the door opposite the sensor button.

Install a button sensor at a casement or awning window similarly, drilling a sensor hole in the hinge side of the jamb for each movable sash. For a double-hung window, install magnetic sensors *(opposite, top)* in the head jamb and in the sill, where a button sensor will corrode and cause false alarms. For sliding windows and doors, recess button sensors in the side jambs.

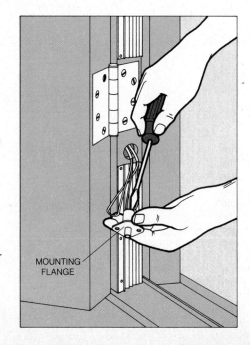

MOUNTING FLANGE

Installing a magnetic sensor. In a convenient spot drill two holes opposite each other in a door or window and its frame, one hole in the edge of the door or window to fit the sensor magnet, one hole in the frame to fit the sensor switch. Fish circuit wires through the frame hole and solder them to the switch leads. Coat the sides of the switch with glue and slide it into the hole, flush with the frame. Glue the magnet into the hole in the door or window.

MAGNET HOLE

SENSOR SWITCH

A Surface-mounted Magnet

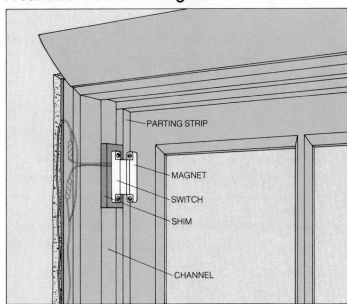

PARTING STRIP

MAGNET

SWITCH

SHIM

CHANNEL

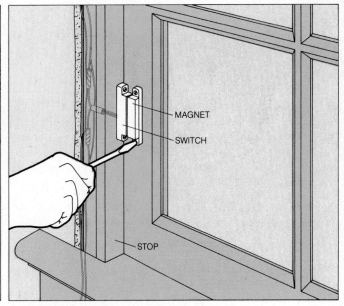

MAGNET

SWITCH

STOP

Arming the outer sash. High in the inner sash channel, nail a wooden shim that is slightly longer than the switch and the same thickness as the parting strip. Drill a ⅜-inch hole through the shim and the jamb, then run circuit wires behind the wall and the casing and through the hole. Connect the wires to the switch, and screw the switch to the shim, leaving enough space between the switch and the sash to accommodate the magnet. Fasten the magnet to the sash directly behind the switch.

For a door or hinged window, mount the sensor close to the unhinged side.

Equipping the inner sash. To install the sensor of the inner sash of a double-hung window, drill a ⅜-inch hole through the window stop and jamb, at least 4 inches above the stool. Run circuit wires behind the wall and the casing (*pages 78-82*) and out the hole. Connect them to the sensor switch and mount it on the stop and next to the sash. Then close the window and screw the sensor magnet to the sash, alongside the switch. Open the window 4 inches and fasten another magnet to the sash opposite the switch. Install a bypass switch (*page 94*) so that you can open the window for ventilation without tripping the alarm.

85

Protection for a Metal Casement

Installing a plunger sensor. Open the window and hold the sensor on the sill near the latch side of the window, with the plunger against the bottom stop. Where the plunger hits the stop, drill a hole that allows the plunger to slide freely through it. With the window closed, push the plunger through the hole and against the sash so that the plunger is fully depressed; mark the sill for mounting screws and, at a location near the terminal screws, for a ⅜-inch hole for the circuit wires. Drill the holes you have marked, then wire and mount the sensor (*inset*).

A Trip-wire Booby Trap

A trip wire for an air conditioner. Fish circuit wires to the window frame low alongside the air conditioner. Screw a spring-loaded retainer to the frame near the wires and connect them to the two terminals. Then insert a nonconducting fiber clip into the retainer. In the air conditioner casing opposite the retainer, drill pilot holes and use sheet-metal screws to mount the spring hanger, taking care not to damage the components inside. Tie a piece of heavy fishing line tautly between the spring and the fiber clip. If the fiber clip is pulled out of the retainer, the circuit closes to sound the alarm.

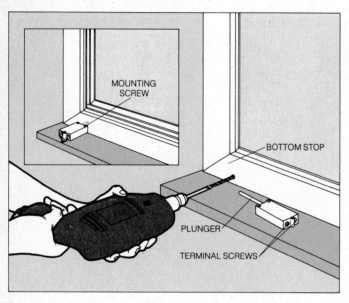

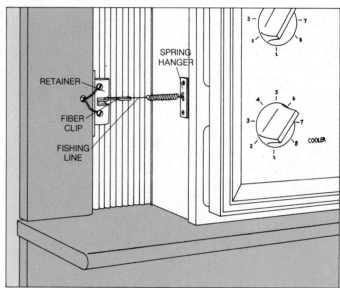

A Mercury Switch for a Tilting Window

1 **Installing the switch.** After fishing circuit wires to the window frame, screw the bracket, with the mercury sensor attached, to the side of the sash. Follow the manufacturer's instructions to mount the sensor for a closed or an open circuit. Then fasten the stationary take-off block on the window frame alongside the sensor. Connect the sensor terminals to each other with a short piece of wire and attach circuit wires to the terminals of the take-off block.

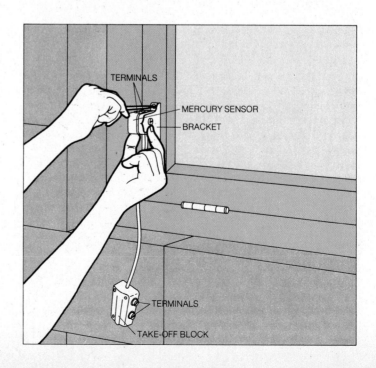

2 **Adjusting the switch.** Raise the window about 2 inches and loosen the adjusting screw on the switch bracket. With a continuity tester connected to the terminals of the take-off block, rotate the sensor until it signals an intrusion—in a closed circuit, the tester light will go out; in an open one, the light will come on. Then turn the sensor back until the continuity tester indicates no intrusion. Tighten the adjusting screw.

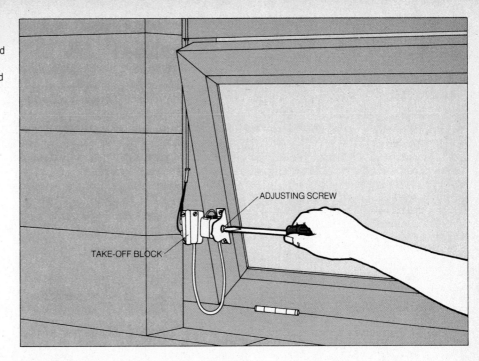

ADJUSTING SCREW

TAKE-OFF BLOCK

Strips of Foil to Signal Window Breakage

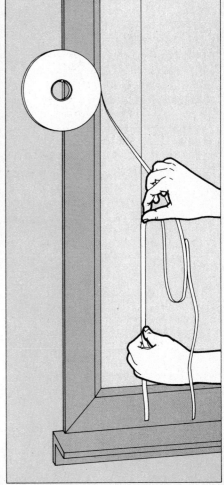

1 **Laying out the foil pattern.** For a window that does not open, such as a picture window, use a grease pencil and a piece of wood or stiff cardboard 3 inches wide to lay out a route for the foil. Working on the outside, start the pattern at the bottom of the window, using the width of the cardboard to draw a line 3 inches from the window frame. Continue around the window to complete the pattern shown in the inset. The beginning and the end of the pattern should be 1½ to 3 inches apart.

Clean the inside of the glass with alcohol and allow it to dry thoroughly.

2 **Applying adhesive-backed foil.** Leaving a 2-inch tail of foil hanging over the window frame, start at one end of the pattern and stick the foil to the inside of the window along the grease-pencil marks on the outside. To do so, peel a few inches of backing paper from the tape—hang the roll of foil from a nail near the window for convenience—stretch it tight and press it against the glass. Smooth any bumps or wrinkles with a matchbook cover. If the foil tears, remove it and start again or, if a break occurs late in the pattern, patch the break with a 6-inch length of foil.

3 **Turning a corner.** At a corner, double the foil back on itself and crease it gently along the intersecting line (*below, left*). Start the foil along the grease-pencil line in the new direction, making a second crease in the corner at a 45° angle (*below, right*). Smooth the foil at the corner with a matchbook cover and continue to apply the foil around the window, stretching it taut and smoothing it flat as you go. Leave a 2-inch tail of foil at the end of the run.

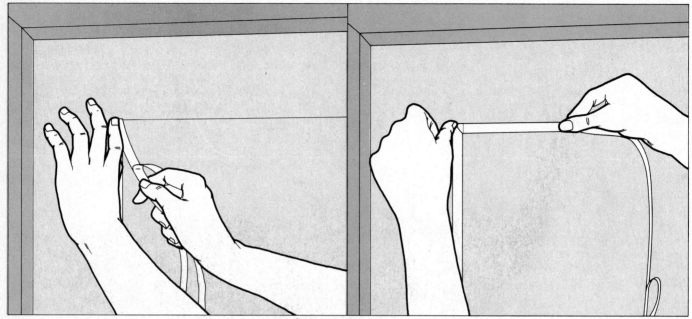

A Connector for Foil on a Movable Door

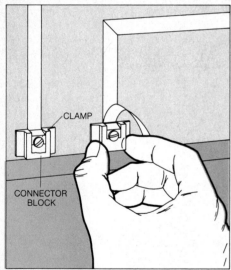

CLAMP

CONNECTOR
BLOCK

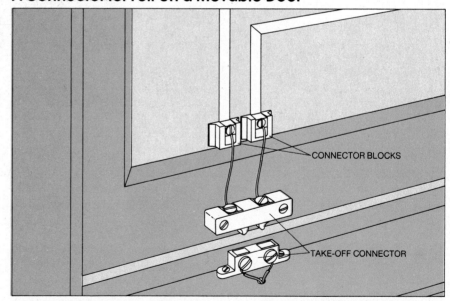

CONNECTOR BLOCKS

TAKE-OFF CONNECTOR

4 **Installing foil-connector blocks.** Pull one end of the foil away from the window edge and double it back so that a connector block will overlap the doubled-back foil ⅛ inch. Stick the adhesive-backed block in place. Remove the screw and clamp from the block, pull the foil over the block and screw down the clamp over the foil; trim excess foil. Install a second block at the other end of the foil; connect circuit wires to the terminal screws on both blocks. Test the circuit.

Coat the tape with foil varnish, available at the foil supplier, to make it brittle and certain to break if the window does. Before varnishing, prick pinholes through any patches in the foil.

Mounting a take-off switch. Through the sill of a double-hung window or through the side frame of a sliding window or door, bore a ⅜-inch hole, then fish circuit wires through it (*pages 78-82*). Install the stationary part of a two-part "take-off connector" on the sill or frame opposite the foil-connector blocks and hook the connector terminals to the circuit wires. With the sash or door closed, mount the movable part of the connector on the sash or door so that its contacts meet those of the stationary connector. Wire the terminals of the movable connector to those of the foil-connector blocks.

For a hinged door or a casement window, install a flexible door cord (*page 95*); wire the cord block on the door to the connector blocks, the circuit wires to the cord block on the wall. On a tilting window, wire the connector blocks to the terminals of a mercury sensor (*pages 86-87*).

Detecting the Step of a Thief

A floor-mat sensor under a rug. Roll back the rug and pad and lay the sensor directly on the floor in the area you wish to protect. If the floor is wood, drill a ¼-inch hole through it into the basement at one end of the mat; fish circuit wires through this hole and connect them to the sensor leads. Under throw rugs, staple sensors in place to prevent slipping, taking care not to staple through the metal contacts.

On a concrete floor, place a sheet of plastic vapor-barrier under the mat and run the circuit wires under a nearby baseboard. Cover the mat with a large throw rug having a nonslip bottom.

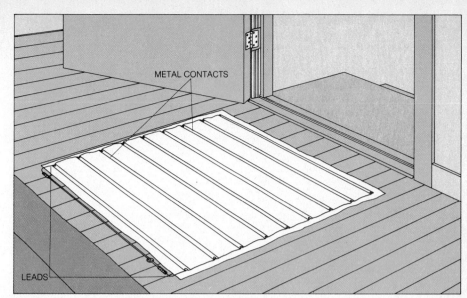

An Invisible Beam to Watch a Passage

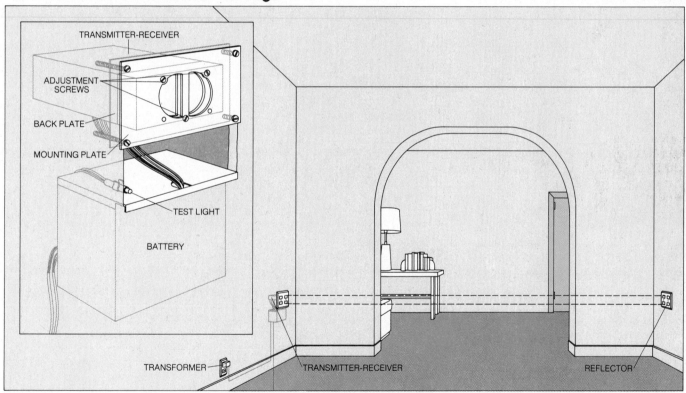

Installing an infrared sensor. Cut a recess for the transmitter-receiver in a wall where its beam has an unobstructed path across a passageway and to the opposite wall, on which the reflector will be mounted. The transmitter-receiver should be at least 1½ feet above the floor—higher if necessary to make the beam pass above tall pets that otherwise would cause false alarms.

Fish two two-conductor cables—one from the control box for the alarm circuit and one from

a nearby electrical outlet to bring power from a plug-in transformer—to the opening. (If power is supplied by the control box, fish a single four-conductor cable from the box to the wall opening.) Fasten cable wires to the coded alarm-circuit and power-circuit terminals on the battery, then hang the battery inside the wall on the lower edge of the opening (insert). Attach the leads from the battery to the color-coded battery terminals on the back of the transmitter-receiver, then clamp the unit to the upper edge and to the

sides of the wall opening, using the mounting plate and the backplate.

Turn on the unit and set the reflector on the opposite wall. Move the reflector until the test light on the battery pack glows, indicating that the beam is striking the reflector. Then use the adjustment screws on the transmitter-receiver to shift the beam, following it with the reflector, until it crosses the passageway you want to monitor. Screw the reflector to the wall.

Sensors for Any Emergency

Although burglary is the danger that stimulates most people to install central alarm systems, fire is a greater threat to life and property. And once you have put in a central fire alarm, you can convert it into a system for all dangers by adding sensors that will detect not only fire but a wide variety of other emergencies—from a flood to a failure of the kitchen freezer.

A centralized fire system is generally better than self-contained alarms. It is usually louder and more reliable. Such a system is adapted to both smoke and heat detectors similar to those in self-contained alarms (page 73). The heat detectors—switches with metal parts that close when heated—are suited to such locations as a furnace room, where a sudden rise in temperature could occur without an open fire.

Most central systems are fitted with fire detectors. Among the other features commonly added are "panic buttons" and a flood detector. You can make a simple flood sensor yourself (opposite, top). A panic button, which allows you to activate the alarm yourself when trouble of any kind threatens, is a simple switch. The easiest to install is a doorbell button that screws directly to window or door casings. If you wish to position the switch on a wall, however, get one mounted on a plate that fits a standard electrical box (opposite, bottom).

Fire and flood sensors as well as panic buttons can be wired into open or closed circuits, but are most often found in open circuits. As explained on page 76, an open circuit does not sound the alarm if a wire breaks or is cut. This tamper-proof feature of a closed circuit—which normally carries current—is unnecessary except where burglary is involved.

There is one disadvantage to an open circuit. If a wire should come loose, the sensors will not work. This drawback is not serious except in the case of fire detectors, where any failure can have fatal consequences. Thus it is best to wire the sensors so that the alarm circuit is monitored for breaks and loose connections. This safety feature requires a "supervised circuit," the control for which is built into many control boxes.

To provide this safeguard, wire all fire sensors on one circuit—not on individual circuits joined at a terminal block (page 97). Then install an end-of-line resistor on the last smoke detector (below, top) or heat sensor (below, bottom) in the circuit. This resistor allows a small current to trickle continuously through the wires. It is too weak to set off the alarm but strong enough to signal the control box that the fire-sensor circuit is working. If this current ceases, the control box buzzes a warning. Should a fire break out, the sensor lets through a much stronger current to the control box, which sounds the alarm.

Warning of Fire or Flood

Wiring open-circuit smoke detectors. Fish a four-conductor cable to the location nearest the control box, pass the cable through the sensor base plate, attach the sensor and connect the wires to the input and output terminals. Attach the red wire to the positive terminal, the black to the negative and the other two wires to the remaining terminals. Similarly connect other sensors to the cable, except the last sensor, which has wires attached only to input terminals. Connect alarm-circuit output terminals of the last sensor with an end-of-line resistor (inset).

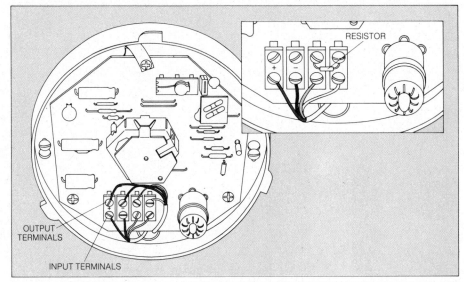

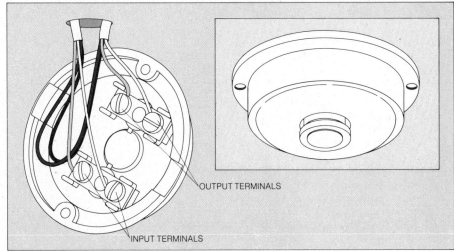

Wiring open-circuit heat sensors. Choose locations and fish cable for heat detectors as explained for smoke detectors (above). At each sensor except the last one, connect only the two alarm-circuit wires to both input and output terminals before you mount the sensor on the ceiling or wall. If the last sensor in the fire loop is a heat detector, connect an end-of-line resistor to the output terminals as shown in the inset above. Screw the sensor in place (inset).

A homemade flood sensor. Near an edge of a piece of plywood, drill holes to fit ¼-inch stove bolts, about ½ inch apart. Then, at each corner of the plywood, hammer upholstery tacks to act as feet. Insert the bolts in the holes from the underside of the sensor and place a washer and a nut over each. Run wires for an open circuit to a low spot on the basement floor and clamp the wires between the nuts and washers. Pour a generous pile of table salt on the floor and position the sensor so that the boltheads rest in the salt. When water rises in the basement and dissolves the salt, the salty water conducts current between the bolts, closing the circuit and triggering the alarm.

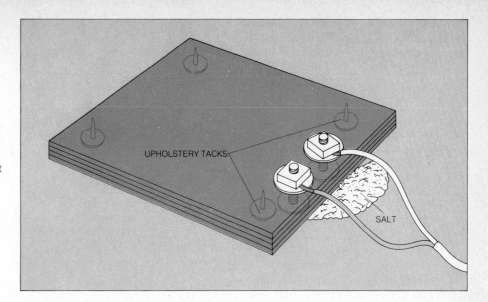

UPHOLSTERY TACKS

SALT

A Panic Button

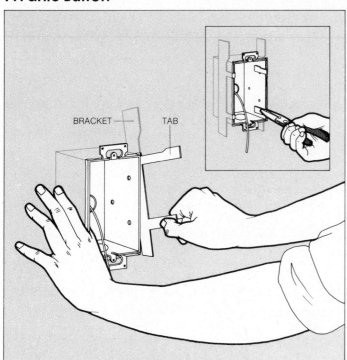

BRACKET — TAB

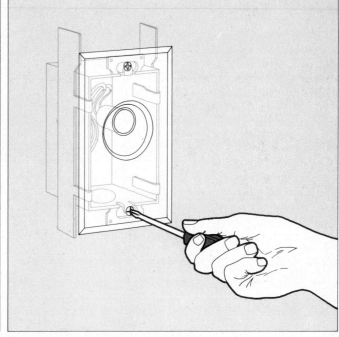

1 Installing a wall box with brackets. Cut a hole in the wall for an electrical box where you want to mount the panic button. Fish circuit wires to the opening and into the box through a hole made by prying out a tab, or knockout. Adjust the ears of the box so that it fits flush with the wall and hold the box in the hole. Slip first the top and then the bottom of a clip known as a madison bracket between one side of the box and the edge of the wall opening. Pull the bracket tight against the inside of the wall and bend the tabs around the edge of the box. In the same way, install a second bracket on the other side of the box. Then tighten the tabs against the box with needle-nose pliers (inset).

2 Connecting the panic button. Solder the circuit wires (page 82) to the terminals on the back of a button switch mounted on a wall plate. Fold the circuit wires gently into the outlet box and screw the switch plate over the box.

Alarm Signals Coded to Identify Dangers

The alarm in an alarm system may be a bell, buzzer, horn, siren or flashing light; the kind you use depends on the danger it is meant to indicate. In an effective system, one type of alarm signal warns of a burglary, another of a fire, so that you can distinguish emergencies by the sound or sight. Most authorities recommend bells both outside and inside a house for burglar alarms, and a horn or siren inside the house for fire alarms. Wire a flood sensor or a "panic button" to sound the burglar alarm.

Interior alarm annunciators generally come on a mounting plate that is simply screwed to the wall; mount the annunciators in or near your bedroom. Most exterior devices come in weather-tight boxes *(right, top)*; mount the box where a burglar cannot easily reach it—under the peak of a gable, for example. For additional security you can install tamper switches inside the box cover and between the box and the wall to set off the alarm if the box is opened or pulled free.

The basic alarms depend on sound, but a flashing light outside helps police identify a house where an alarm is sounding. For this purpose a strobe—similar to those used for flash photography—is mounted on or near the alarm box, where it can be seen from the street, and wired to flash when the alarm sounds.

Wiring strobe lights and other signaling devices is simple. You link their wires—generally 18-gauge two-conductor cable—to wires leading from the control panel, using either soldered joints *(page 83)* or terminal blocks *(right, bottom)*. Strobes and most sirens must be wired according to positive and negative polarity, with red wires running to positive terminals or other red wires, and black wires running to negative terminals or other black wires. In a circuit without a light or a siren, you can generally wire a bell without observing polarity.

Installing an Exterior Alarm

1 **Attaching a strobe to the box.** Using the mounting holes in the strobe housing as a template, mark locations for screw holes on the box cover, then drill four ³/₁₆-inch holes through the cover and an additional hole through its center for the wires. Screw the strobe to the box.

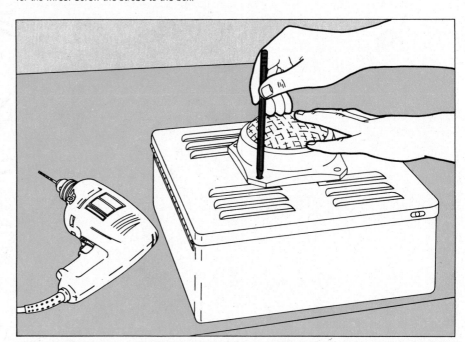

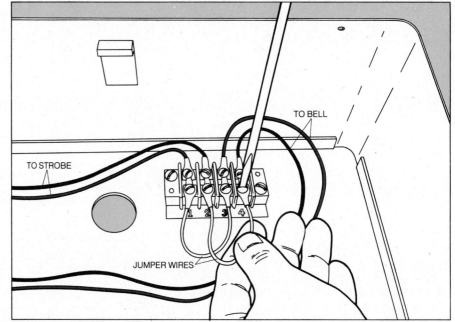

2 **Linking the strobe and the bell.** Connect the red strobe wire to the No. 1 terminal inside the box, the black strobe wire to the No. 2 terminal, the red bell wire to the No. 3 terminal and the black bell wire to the No. 4 terminal. Install jumper wires between terminals 1 and 3 and between terminals 2 and 4. In this example, connections are made with flat lugs crimped onto the ends of the wires and slipped under the terminal screws.

3 Mounting the box. Inside the house, fish two-conductor 18-gauge cable from the control-panel location to a point on an inside wall corresponding to the box location (*pages 78-82*) and drill a ¼-inch hole through the wall at that point; then, from outside, screw the box to the wall, lining up the large hole in the back of the box with the hole you have drilled. Pull the control-panel cable through the hole, and connect the red wire to the No. 1 terminal inside the box and the black wire to the No. 2 terminal (*inset*). Close and secure the cover.

If you would like to use outside and inside bells in the same circuit, splice the wires of the outside bell to the wires running between the inside bell and the control panel, using wire caps or soldered splices and matching red wires to red, black wires to black.

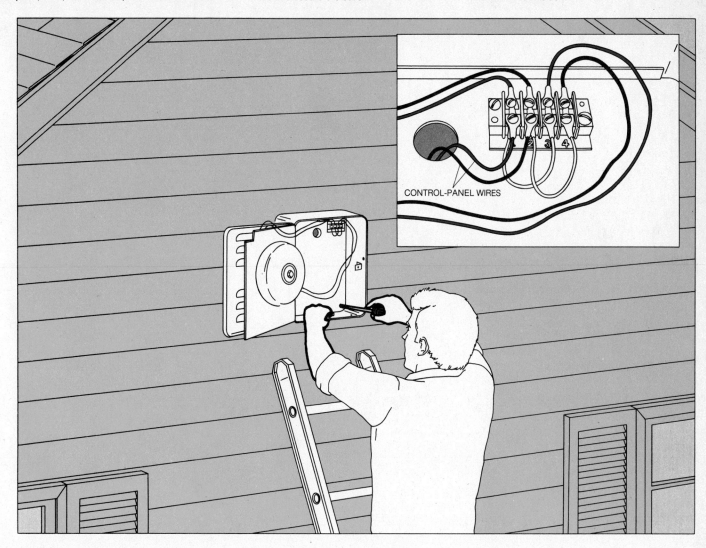

CONTROL-PANEL WIRES

A Telephone Dialer for Peace of Mind—at a Price

An automatic telephone dialer, which sends a prerecorded alarm message to the police or fire station, is an effective weapon against a burglar who disables conventional signaling devices, or a fire that breaks out in a homeowner's absence. However, false alarms are almost inevitable in any system, and they become a special problem when every one is transmitted directly to authorities. Some police and fire departments are so harried by false dialer alarms that they may ignore dialer calls or levy a fine if they answer a false alarm. Despite this potential drawback, a dialer may be essential in a home located so far from neighbors that a conventional alarm cannot be seen or heard by them.

Dialers are expensive, but they are also ingenious and versatile. Some models can be programed to call several different numbers with different messages; others repeat a message until the tape runs out—if the call is put on hold, the message can still get through when the call is finally answered. One sophisticated model can monitor the condition of the phone lines, sounding an alarm if they are cut. A so-called "line-seizing" feature on some dialers enables the device to override incoming calls and to make calls even if the phone is left off the hook.

Controls and Switches: The Brains of the System

Directly or indirectly, every component of a comprehensive alarm system is wired to the control box, which powers the system, receives signals from sensors, sends signals to alarms, and switches all or part of the system on and off.

Preassembled control boxes, like the one on pages 98-99, come with eight to 30 separate terminals to handle these connections. Control switches generally are not located at the box itself, though an alarm system can be armed and disarmed—made operative or inoperative—at its control box. More often, for convenience and practicality, several control switches are scattered around the house.

The simplest kind of control is independent of the control box. It is a bypass switch *(below)*, which, when turned to the "off" position, disconnects a single sensor—to permit you to open a window, perhaps, or shut off one infrared sensor *(page 89)* without affecting the rest of the system. More complex switches—professionals call them remote-control stations—turn the system on or off.

Near vulnerable entrances and windows, control stations should be key-operated. (For control stations in more secure locations, a push-button switch is adequate.) One of the simplest *(opposite)* goes directly into a door; a more complex type *(page 96)* has an indicator light and a built-in tamper switch.

A switch designed for use inside a house comes in a plastic housing for installation in a standard outlet box, and most models have two indicator lights. A green light glows when the system is on stand-by and ready to be armed, with all sensor-equipped doors and windows properly closed; a red light means the system is armed. Indicator lights using light-emitting diodes (LEDs) rather than incandescent bulbs last far longer.

Installing a Bypass Switch

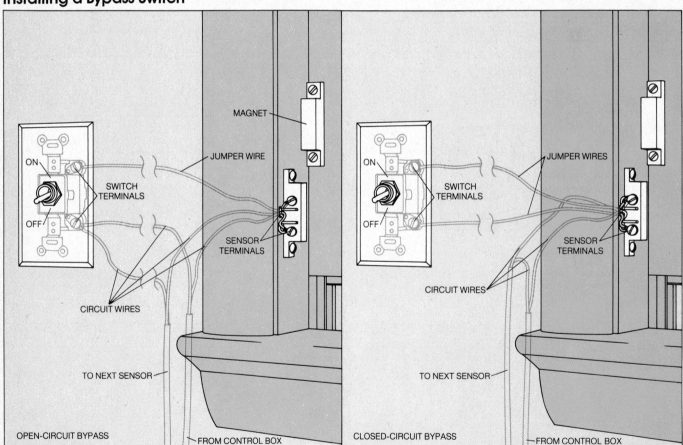

OPEN-CIRCUIT BYPASS   CLOSED-CIRCUIT BYPASS

Wiring the switch. For an open-circuit system *(page 76)*, a connector wire and a toggle switch disconnect a sensor such as the magnetic window device illustrated at bottom left. (For contrast, an open-circuit sensor without a bypass is shown on page 76.) Connect one circuit wire of the two-conductor 18-gauge cable commonly used in this kind of installation to one switch terminal; the other circuit wire is connected to one sensor terminal. Connect the remaining switch terminal to the other sensor terminal.

To bypass a sensor in a closed-circuit system such as the one on page 77, use jumpers to connect both terminals of a toggle switch to both sensor terminals *(right)*.

If you are wiring a system of open-circuit sensors, position the switch assembly so that the lever points up toward the ON marking when the bypass is in the "on" position; if your system uses closed-circuit sensors, turn the switch upside down inside its plastic housing. In both types of circuit the lettering on the housing will then correctly indicate the setting of the bypass.

A Key Switch in an Entry Door

1 Drilling the mounting holes. From outside the door, drill a 1-inch hole through it, 4 inches in from the hinge side. Then, using the faceplate of the switch assembly as a template, drill two ³/₁₆-inch holes ¼ inch deep into the door.

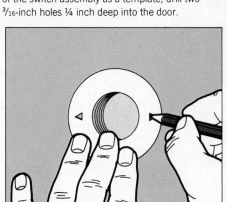

2 Installing the switch. Solder 3-inch-long wires to the terminals at the back of the switch assembly. Then slide the faceplate against the dial face and insert the assembly in the door, pushing the triangular stops on the back of the faceplate into the ³/₁₆-inch holes. While you hold the assembly in place, have a helper inside the house slide a washer over the switch assembly and secure the assembly in the door by screwing the end cap on (right).

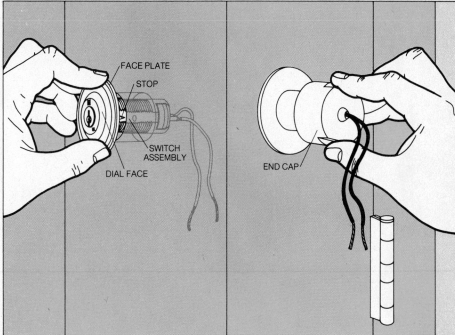

FACE PLATE
STOP
SWITCH ASSEMBLY
DIAL FACE
END CAP

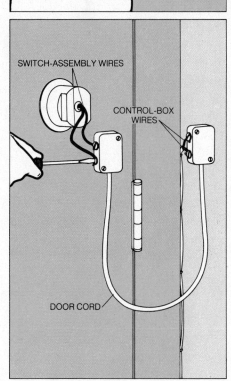

SWITCH-ASSEMBLY WIRES
CONTROL-BOX WIRES
DOOR CORD

3 Installing the cord assembly. Screw one door-cord terminal block to the door just below the end cap and fasten the other block to the wall beyond the jamb. Connect the switch wires to the block on the door and connect the control-box wires to the block on the wall.

A Key Switch in a Doorjamb

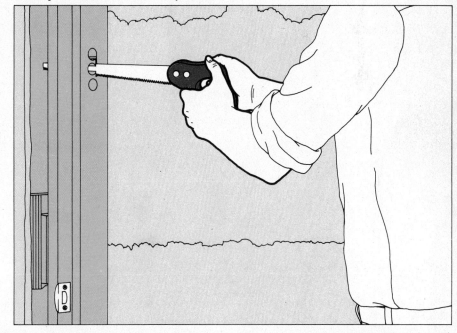

1 Cutting the mounting hole. Pry the interior casing off at the knob side of the door (page 23) and cut a long, oval hole in the jamb for the switch. To mark the hole, use the backplate—the mounting plate for the lock, the light and the tamper switch—as a template, then drill holes inside the mark and saw out the remaining wood. At the bottom of the shim space between the doorjamb and the rough frame, drill a ³/₈-inch hole through the floor and fish five-conductor wire for the switch through the floor and the hole you have drilled in the jamb.

2 **Soldering the wires.** Use the nuts supplied by the manufacturer to mount the lock, tamper switch and light on the backplate, then tape the plate to the jamb, with the electrical terminals facing out. Solder any two cable wires (both colored gray here for clarity and simplicity) to the tamper-switch terminals, a white wire from the cable to one of the light terminals, a white jumper wire to the other light terminal, two black cable wires to the key-switch terminals, and the free end of the jumper wire to either key-switch terminal.

3 **Securing the backplate and cover plate.** Untape the backplate, insert the lock, light and tamper-switch barrels into the holes in the jamb and fasten the backplate to the doorjamb with wood screws. Use short machine screws to secure the plastic front cover.

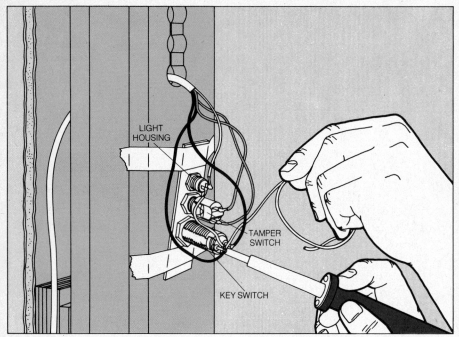

An Interior Key Switch

Wiring the switch. Run five-conductor wire from the control box to a standard outlet box (*page 91*) installed at a convenient location on a wall. Tape the mounting plate to the wall with the terminals facing out, and solder the connections for the key switch and the red light as shown above left; solder the two gray cable wires to the green-light terminals.

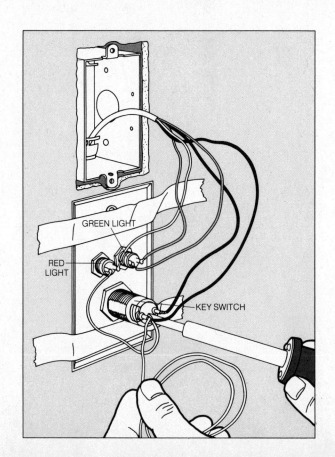

Wiring the Control Box

You can gauge the capacity and sophistication of most control boxes by simply counting the terminals inside. The simplest box is likely to contain at least eight terminals, serving four distinct types of circuit: an open burglary-sensor circuit, a closed burglary-sensor circuit, a circuit for a bell and a strobe light, and a circuit for a disarming switch.

Beyond this minimum, a box may contain 20 or more terminals for such features as fire sensors, fire horns, tamper switches to warn of sabotage attempts, indicator lights, panic buttons to let you set off alarms and a telephone dialer to summon police or firemen automatically.

Buy a box large enough to handle any circuits you may want to add in the future, and be sure that the box you buy can handle fire detectors, if you intend to use them—some require a constant trickle of current from the control box for their operation *(page 90)*.

Whatever its size, the box you buy will run on 120-volt house current, stepped down by a transformer to the 6 or 12 volts used in the alarm system. A more sophisticated model contains a continuously recharging battery—preferably a gel-cell or lead-oxide type—to power the system if house current fails. Wiring the control box involves a maze of wires and cables, but requires patience rather than special skill. The procedure is the same for all boxes, although terminal arrangements inside may vary from the typical model illustrated on pages 98 and 99.

2 Wiring the blocks to the control box. Cut four wires long enough to reach from the jumper-wire sides of the terminal blocks to the terminals inside the control box. For the closed circuits, connect two wires to the free terminals at the first and last circuits. For the open circuit, connect wires to the two jumper-wire terminals closest to the control box. Thread all four wires through a knockout hole at the top of the box and use the same hole or nearby holes for all sensor, alarm and control-switch wires.

1 Wiring the terminal blocks. Attach the two leads from each open burglary-sensor circuit to pairs of adjacent terminals on one side of a terminal block mounted next to the control box; attach the leads from closed circuits to another block. On the remaining side of the open-circuit terminal block, connect alternate terminals, using two long jumpers stripped of ½ inch of insulation every 1½ inches: wrap the stripped sections of the wires around the alternate terminal screws and tighten them. On the unwired side of the closed-circuit terminal block, connect adjacent terminals so that one wire from each sensor circuit is linked to one wire of the next.

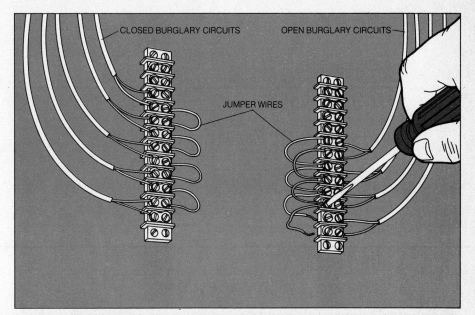

CLOSED BURGLARY CIRCUITS   OPEN BURGLARY CIRCUITS

JUMPER WIRES

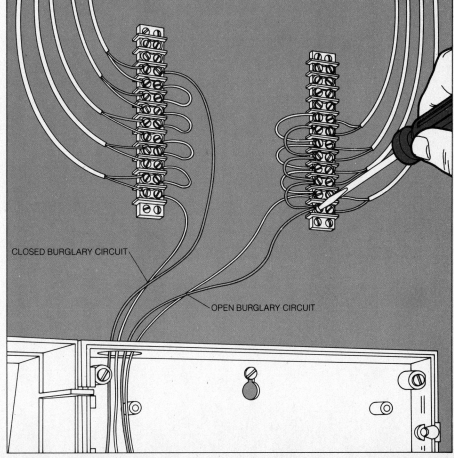

CLOSED BURGLARY CIRCUIT

OPEN BURGLARY CIRCUIT

3 Wiring the sensor circuits. Following the manufacturer's instructions, generally provided in a diagram inside the control-box cover, attach the wires of the two burglary circuits to their terminals. (In this model the terminals consist of clamps and setscrews, and are designed to accept two or more wires; if your model has simple screw terminals, twist and solder wires together before making the connection.)

Smoke-detector circuits *(page 90)* are linked to the control box through a four-conductor cable. Attach the two sensor wires of these circuits to their terminals. The red and black wires go to terminals marked either AUXILIARY POWER or SMOKE-DETECTOR POWER, which are coded for polarity; attach the red wire to the positive terminal, and the black wire to the negative terminal.

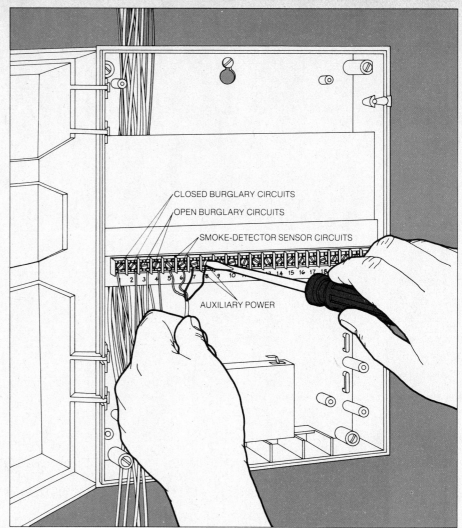

CLOSED BURGLARY CIRCUITS
OPEN BURGLARY CIRCUITS
SMOKE-DETECTOR SENSOR CIRCUITS
AUXILIARY POWER

4 Wiring the alarm circuits. Observing polarity, connect the wires for the burglar- and fire-alarm circuits *(pages 92-93)* to the terminals assigned to them in the box, red wires on the positive terminals, black wires on the negative.

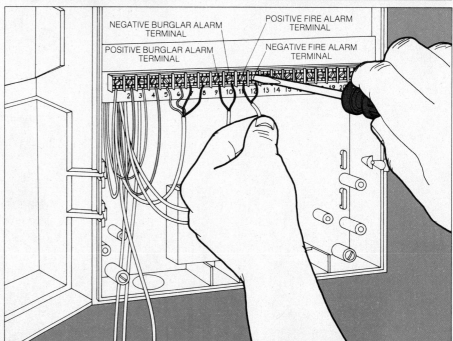

NEGATIVE BURGLAR ALARM TERMINAL
POSITIVE FIRE ALARM TERMINAL
POSITIVE BURGLAR ALARM TERMINAL
NEGATIVE FIRE ALARM TERMINAL

5 **Wiring control-station circuits.** A remote-control station mounted on a doorjamb outside the house (*pages 95-96*) is linked to the control box with a five-conductor cable. Connect the two gray wires of the cable to the tamper-switch terminals, and the two black wires to the key-switch terminals. In this typical box, a red indicator-light circuit shares one terminal with the key switch and has one independent terminal; connect the white wire to the independent red-light terminal.

To wire the five-conductor cable of the corresponding control station inside the house (*page 96*), attach black wires to the key-switch terminals, gray wires to the green-light terminals and the white wire to the independent red-light terminal (*inset*).

A remote-control station in a door (*page 95*) is wired with a two-conductor cable; attach the black wires to the key-switch terminals.

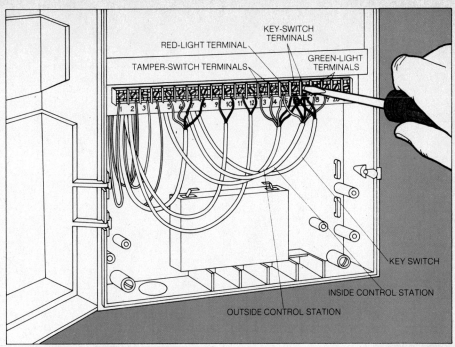

RED-LIGHT TERMINAL
KEY-SWITCH TERMINALS
TAMPER-SWITCH TERMINALS
GREEN-LIGHT TERMINALS
KEY SWITCH
INSIDE CONTROL STATION
OUTSIDE CONTROL STATION

6 **Hooking up power.** Attach the red battery wire from the back of the terminal strip inside the box to the positive terminal of the battery, and the black battery wire to the negative terminal. Attach a two-conductor cable to the transformer terminals in the box, run the cable through a knockout hole and attach the other ends of the wires to the terminals at the base of the transformer. Plug the transformer into a receptacle, with the transformer mounting tab secured behind the screw at the center of the receptacle cover plate, and switch on the system.

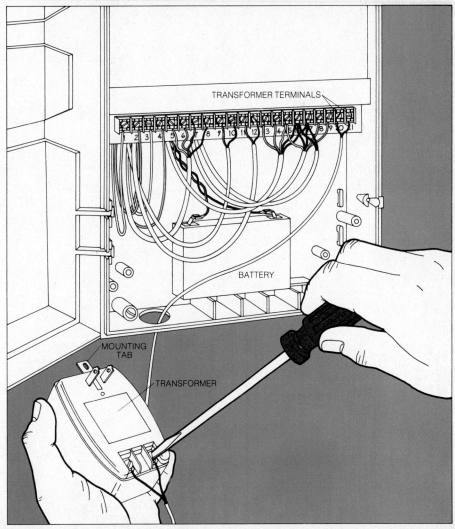

TRANSFORMER TERMINALS
BATTERY
MOUNTING TAB
TRANSFORMER

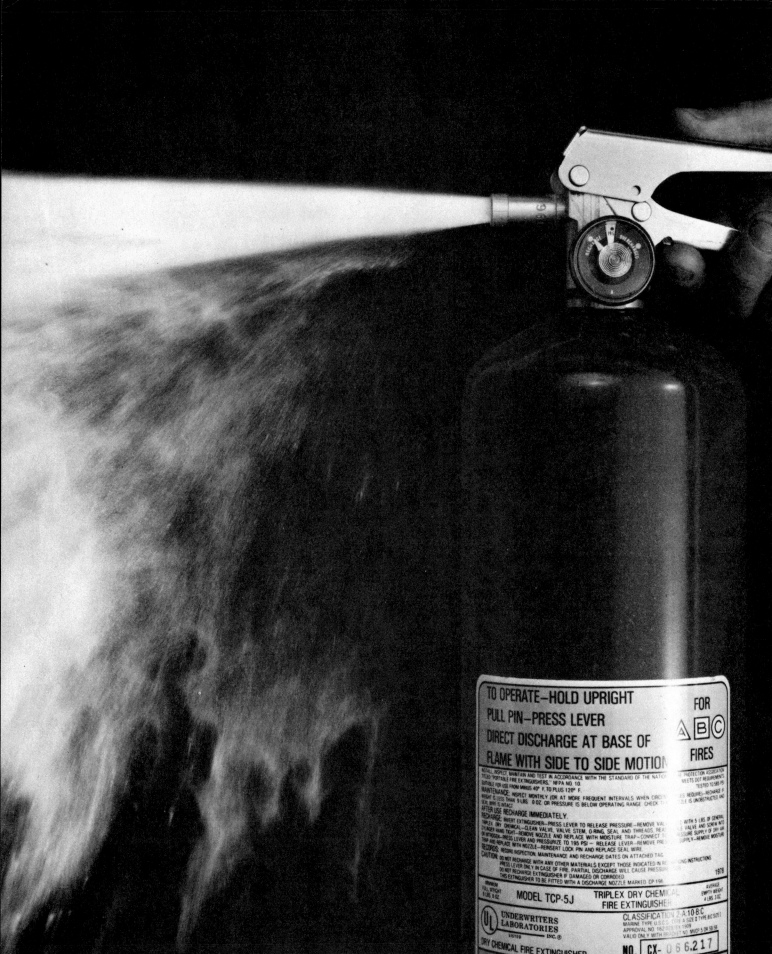

TO OPERATE—HOLD UPRIGHT
PULL PIN—PRESS LEVER
DIRECT DISCHARGE AT BASE OF
FLAME WITH SIDE TO SIDE MOTION

FOR
△ⒷⒸ
FIRES

INSTALL, INSPECT, MAINTAIN AND TEST IN ACCORDANCE WITH THE STANDARD OF THE NATION... FIRE PROTECTION ASSOCIATION. "PORTABLE FIRE EXTINGUISHERS," NFPA NO. 10. MEETS DOT REQUIREMENTS. SUITABLE FOR USE FROM MINUS 40° F. TO PLUS 120° F. TESTED TO 585 PSI

MAINTENANCE: INSPECT MONTHLY (OR AT MORE FREQUENT INTERVALS WHEN CIRCU... ...ES REQUIRE)—RECHARGE IF WEIGHT IS LESS THAN 9 LBS. 0 OZ. OR PRESSURE IS BELOW OPERATING RANGE. CHECK T... ...ZLE IS UNOBSTRUCTED AND SEAL WIRE IS INTACT.
AFTER USE RECHARGE IMMEDIATELY.
RECHARGE: INVERT EXTINGUISHER—PRESS LEVER TO RELEASE PRESSURE—REMOVE VAL... ...WITH 5 LBS. OF GENERAL TRIPLEX DRY CHEMICAL—CLEAN VALVE, VALVE STEM, O-RING, SEAL AND THREADS. REA... ...E VALVE AND SCREW INTO CYLINDER HAND TIGHT—REMOVE NOZZLE AND REPLACE WITH MOISTURE TRAP—CONNECT T... ...PRESSURE SUPPLY OF DRY AIR OR NITROGEN—PRESS LEVER AND PRESSURIZE TO 195 PSI — RELEASE LEVER—REMOVE PRES... ...SUPPLY—REMOVE MOISTURE TRAP AND REPLACE WITH NOZZLE—REINSERT LOCK PIN AND REPLACE SEAL WIRE.
RECORDS: RECORD INSPECTION, MAINTENANCE AND RECHARGE DATES ON ATTACHED TAG
CAUTION: DO NOT RECHARGE WITH ANY OTHER MATERIALS EXCEPT THOSE INDICATED IN RE... ...ING INSTRUCTIONS
PRESS LEVER ONLY IN CASE OF FIRE. PARTIAL DISCHARGE WILL CAUSE PRESSUR... ...
DO NOT RECHARGE EXTINGUISHER IF DAMAGED OR CORRODED
THIS EXTINGUISHER TO BE FITTED WITH A DISCHARGE NOZZLE MARKED CP 196 ...   1978

FULL WEIGHT
9 LBS. 8 OZ.

MODEL TCP-5J

TRIPLEX DRY CHEMICAL
FIRE EXTINGUISHER

AVERAGE
EMPTY WEIGHT
4 LBS. 8 OZ.

ⓊⓁ UNDERWRITERS
LABORATORIES
INC.®
LISTED

CLASSIFICATION 2-A:10-B:C
MARINE TYPE U.S.C.G. TYPE A SIZE II TYPE B:C SIZE I
APPROVAL NO. 162.028/EX-1909
VALID ONLY WITH BRACKET NO. MVO-5 OR 5B-16

DRY CHEMICAL FIRE EXTINGUISHER

NO. CX- 0 6 6,2 1 7

Defenses against Fire

A burst of fire-taming dust. When the handle of a dry chemical fire extinguisher is squeezed, a stream of dust squirts toward the fire. Aimed at the base of the flames, the powder forms a blanket that smothers the blaze. Dry chemical extinguishers are effective on most kinds of fires, but other types of extinguishers *(pages 108-109)* have specialized uses.

Building codes and electrical codes specify standards for home construction that make houses relatively fireproof. For example, regulations in the United States now require the wall between a house and an attached garage to be covered on the garage side with wallboard; in former years, there was no such requirement and a fire in the garage could spread rapidly to the main part of the house. In the case of a house with balloon framing, a type of construction that normally incorporates no cross members between studs, fires once raced from the bottom of the house to the top in a few minutes; nowadays, codes demand that balloon framing include such cross members.

Even today, codes do not require builders to avoid every hazardous design or to incorporate all the safety features that can reduce the probability of fire, inhibit its spread once it starts, and make the house easier to escape from. A master bedroom situated away from children's bedrooms, for example, offers a peaceful retreat for parents but may make it impossible for them to reach children in the event of a fire. Bedroom windows that are set high above the floor offer desirable privacy—but no child and few adults would be able to escape a fire through them.

Lower windows are not easy to install, but many other hazards built into an existing home can be remedied fairly simply. Nailing wallboard to garage walls *(pages 105-106)* is an elementary job, fire stops can be added to a balloon-frame house *(page 104)* and flammable draperies can be flameproofed *(pages 102-103)*. If the door at the top of the basement stairs is the old-fashioned paneled type or the modern, inexpensive hollow-core flush type, replace it with a solid-core flush door, which retards the spread of flames much better than the others. If there is no door to close off basement stairs, install one. And common-sense safeguards, such as small extinguishers *(left)*, should be added to household equipment.

One special hazard may affect about two million homes built between 1965 and 1973. They contain wiring made from aluminum rather than the copper used before and since. Aluminum wiring is safe if it is used with devices—mainly switches and receptacles—that are designed for it. But it can cause overheating and fire if it is connected to devices meant for copper wiring, a dangerous mistake that was committed by many ill-informed builders. You can tell if you have aluminum wiring in your house by looking inside switch and receptacle boxes; its wires are silvery instead of copper-colored. If you discover aluminum wiring, examine the switches and receptacles; if they are not marked CO-ALR (stamped on 15- and 20-ampere devices) or CU-AL (on devices in higher-amperage circuits), replace them with switches and receptacles that are so marked.

Easy Ways to Make Your House Hard to Burn

Once in every generation, the average American family can expect to summon the fire department. And each year about 7,800 people die in home fires. Monetary damages average well over two billion dollars annually. Much of this tragic loss could be avoided by common-sense living habits and simple alterations in house structures and furnishings.

Fire hazards concentrate in certain parts of the house—not necessarily in the way you might expect. Kitchen fires, fueled by grease in overheated pans or inside exhaust fans, are the most common. Numerous as they are, such blazes account for only 14 per cent of fire fatalities, because someone is usually present to extinguish the flames.

Fires in living rooms, although they amount to only 12 per cent of all house fires, account for 39 per cent of the fatalities. Most are caused by smokers who fall asleep, allowing glowing embers to drop onto sofa and chair cushions. Ignorance causes other fires. The heat from the electronic innards of television sets, for example, has started fires when sets were left on overnight or operated on a carpeted floor—the pile can block cooling vents under the set.

Fires like this can usually be prevented by following the instructions that come with appliances and by observing the safety rules drilled into everyone from childhood. But not even the most vigilant can guard against fires set by lightning bolts, exploding gas mains or, in some regions, brush fires. One recent California brush fire destroyed 266 houses, valued at $21 million.

Though you cannot guarantee that your house will not catch fire, you can make it harder for a fire to spread. Begin by taking stock of your home furnishings. Current consumer-protection laws require all mattresses and carpeting to be made flame-resistant, but draperies and older mattresses and carpets generally are not treated.

You can add such protection yourself with fire-retardant solutions mixed from chemicals bought from chemical-supply houses or drugstores. The recipes in the chart (opposite, top) are intended for materials containing cellulose: vegetable-fiber fabrics such as cotton, rayon or linen, alone or blended with synthetics; wallpaper, including the kind made with grass; and even Christmas trees. Pure synthetics such as nylon and animal-fiber fabrics such as silk and wool resist flame without treatment. The solutions are not harmful and will not discolor fabrics. They are meant for furnishings, which are cleaned rarely if at all; washing removes the protection.

But the furnishings of a house are not the only danger. The walls of some houses, for example, may lack fire stops to block the upward spread of fire. A few lengths of 2-by-4 can remedy this situation (page 104). Some building materials can spread fire rapidly from one room to another. Use the chart below to determine which materials are safest.

If a wall or ceiling is finished in a flammable material—or, like some garage walls, not finished at all (pages 105-106)—the only good remedy is replacement with safer materials. For extra protection you can use "intumescent" paint, which reacts to the heat of a fire by puffing up into a layer of insulation. Among several brands are Flamort, Everseal and Ocean Chemical.

A fire that attacks from outside the house is more difficult to defend against. But in brush-fire country, such as Southern California, there is a way to make a house less likely to burn. Simply clear easily ignited vegetation from around the house with a scythe and replace it with lawn and fire-resistant plants (opposite, bottom). In a protective green belt around the house, these plants can help to hold a brush fire at bay.

Fire Ratings for Building Materials

Flame-Spread Rating	Wall or Ceiling Material
Class A (0-25)—Excellent	Masonry
	Glass
	Plaster
	Type X gypsum wallboard
	Flame-resistant acoustical ceiling tile
	Fire-rated fiberboard
	Asbestos-cement board
Class B (26-75)—Good	Most gypsum wallboard
	Pressure-treated wood
Class C (76-200)—Fair	Hardboard
	Particle board
	Most plywood
	Most solid wood, 1 inch thick
	Most acoustical ceiling tile
	Fire-rated wall paneling
Class D (over 200)—Poor	Unrated fiberboard
	Unrated wall paneling

Picking a safe material. Common coverings for walls and ceilings are grouped into four classes by "flame-spread ratings." Established by the National Bureau of Standards and national testing laboratories, these ratings are based on a comparison of the materials' burning speeds with those of asbestos (specified as zero) and dry red oak (100). Class A and B materials are recommended by fire-prevention experts for halls, stairways, kitchens and utility rooms. Except in these locations, Class C materials may be used to cover small areas, but not an entire room. Class D materials are unsuitable for home use; they do not meet minimum standards of the federal government. Manufacturers of building materials mark many of their products, including acoustical ceiling tiles and wall paneling, with flame-spread ratings.

Flame-proofing Recipes

Mixing and applying the chemicals. The fire-retarding solutions in the chart are prepared by dissolving the ingredients in the quantity of hot tap water called for in the recipe.

To treat fabrics and paper products, wet them thoroughly with the appropriate solution by spraying or dipping, then allow them to dry flat. To treat a Christmas tree, spray or paint the tops and undersides of branches with the water-glass solution. Let the tree dry, then treat it again to ensure that each needle and branch is coated with a shiny, fire-retardant glaze.

Material to be Treated	Recipe
Permanent-press fabrics (blends of vegetable and synthetic fibers)	12 ounces diammonium phosphate 2 quarts water
Untreated vegetable-fiber fabrics	7 ounces borax 3 ounces boric acid 2 quarts water
Paper and cardboard	7 ounces borax 3 ounces boric acid 5 ounces diammonium phosphate 1 teaspoon liquid dishwashing detergent 3½ quarts water
Christmas tree	4½ gallons sodium silicate (water glass) 2 quarts water 2 teaspoons liquid dishwashing detergent

Plantings for Brush-fire Country

Type of Plant	Plant Name
Ground Covers	Rosea ice plant (*Drosanthemum hispidum*) Jelly beans (*Sedum rubrotinctum*) Trailing gazania (*Gazania uniflora*) Trailing African daisy (*Osteospermum fruticosum*) Kentucky bluegrass (*Poa pratensis*) Rye grass (*Lolium*, several species) White clover (*Trifolium repens*)
Shrubs	Oleander (*Nerium oleander*) Elephant bush (*Portulacaria afra 'variegata'*) Bluechalksticks (*Senecio serpens*) Toyon (*Heteromeles arbutifolia*) Common lilac (*Syringa vulgaris*)
Trees	Gum trees (*Eucalyptus*, several species) Carob (*Ceratonia siliqua*) California pepper (*Schinus molle*) California laurel (*Umbellularia californica*) Cottonwood (*Populus deltoides*)

Selecting the plants. The foliage plants listed at left are naturally fire-resistant—some contain as much as 95 per cent water—and all thrive in warm, arid regions where brush fires occur. Plant the yard within 100 feet of the house with ground covers from the chart, which includes three of the most popular lawn grasses. Add shrubs and trees for accent but plant them no closer than 30 feet from the house and no less than 18 feet apart so that a fire cannot jump easily from one to the next and then to the house.

Building Walls that Resist Fire

Nowadays, new homes generally contain two built-in barriers to the spread of fire: horizontal 2-by-4 fire stops inside the walls, to block flames that shoot up the natural chimneys between the studs; and fire-resistant walls to block fires that might otherwise spread from an attached garage. Many older homes lack fire stops, and many built shortly after World War II lack protection against garage fires. In these homes a fire can race from a basement to an attic or from a garage to a bedroom in less than three minutes.

To find out whether your house has fire stops, shine a flashlight up into the exterior walls from the basement or crawl space. If you see the bottom of a plywood subfloor and cannot see the wall studs of the story above, your house has inherently fire-resistant "platform-frame" construction. Each story has its own walls, and the horizontal top and bottom plates of the walls serve as fire stops. (Some platform-frame houses also have horizontal 2-by-4s between studs, 4 feet from the floor, but these are added for structural reasons rather than fire safety.)

If you can see the wall studs, your house has balloon framing, common until 1930 and still used occasionally today. A balloon-frame house has long studs that run uninterrupted from the foundation to the roof; the spaces between studs should be blocked at the top and bottom of each story by fire stops, visible from under the floor. If the spaces in your house are open, nail new fire stops level with the first floor (below, top); if the first-story studs are exposed, or if you are willing to remove a strip of the wall covering, nail additional fire stops behind the ledger board that supports the second-floor joists (below, bottom).

Homes built after 1960 generally have walls of fire-resisting gypsum wallboard between an attached garage and the rest of the house. If yours does not, nail a layer of wallboard to one or both sides of each wall, either directly to the studs or over the existing wall covering; replace the door between the house and the garage with a solid-core model. If a second story lies over the garage, nail wallboard to the garage ceiling as well.

Ordinary wallboard has some fire resistance, but for this job use Type X wallboard, a slightly more expensive variety specifically designed for fire walls. The gypsum in the core of Type X wallboard contains, in its crystal structure, 50 per cent water by volume; when the wallboard is exposed to heat, the gypsum crystals gradually release the water as steam, holding back fire for nearly 30 minutes. Available in ½- and ⅝-inch thicknesses, sheets of Type X wallboard generally measure 4 by 8 feet; longer lengths can be ordered. The sheets usually are installed vertically, like ordinary wallboard; the edges can be concealed with paper tape and premixed joint compound where appearance is important, but this does not add to fire resistance.

To prepare the walls, move the electrical switches and receptacles outward slightly, and nail strips of lumber to the doorjamb, so that both the jambs and the electrical fixtures will be flush with the face of the wallboard. If any ducts or pipes run through the wall, frame them with 2-by-4s to provide nailing surfaces for the wallboard (page 106).

Adding Fire Stops to a Balloon-frame House

Installing the fire stops. For a basement or crawl space (top), cut lumber as wide and thick as the studs into blocks that fit horizontally between each pair of studs. Tap the blocks into position, against the floor above, and toenail them to the studs. If joists lie next to studs, cut the blocks to fit between the joists and studs.

At the top of the first-story wall (bottom), tap blocks up behind the ledger board that supports the second-floor joists and drive eightpenny nails through the ledger board into the blocks.

Putting Up Gypsum Wallboard

Putting up the sheets. Mark the center of each stud on the ceiling and floor. Place a sheet of wallboard against the studs at one end of the wall and push the sheet tight against the ceiling with a foot-operated lever, such as a wedge-shaped piece of wood on a scrap of pipe. Align the edge of the sheet with the center of a stud and drive several 1⅝-inch ring-shanked nails through the wallboard into the studs. The final hammer blow should set each nail about $1/32$ inch below the surface and make a gentle depression, or "dimple," around the nailhead, without tearing the paper face of the wallboard.

Working from the center of the sheet outward to the edges, drive pairs of nails into each stud every 12 inches, with the second nail in each pair 2 inches from the first. Drive single nails every 8 inches around the edges of the sheet, about ⅜ inch from the edge.

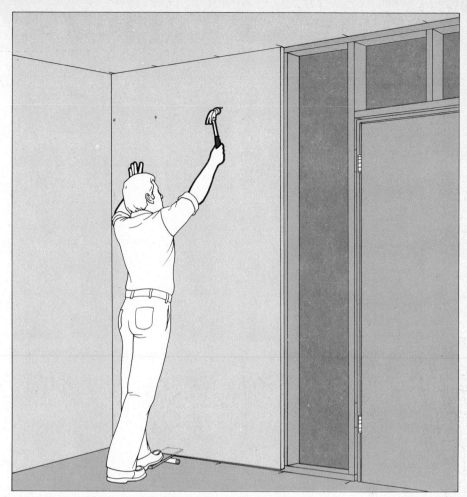

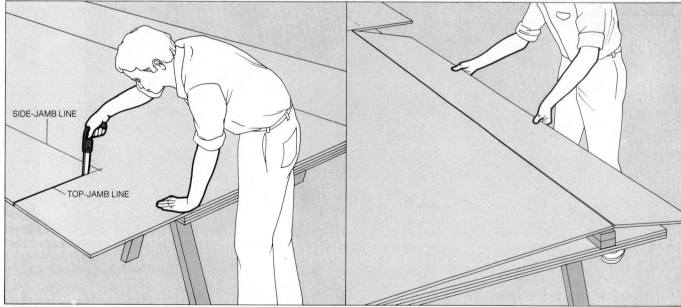

SIDE-JAMB LINE

TOP-JAMB LINE

Fitting wallboard around a door. Measure from the ceiling to the top of the side jamb nearest the installed sheet of wallboard, then measure from the edge of this sheet to the top and bottom of the side jamb. Subtract ¼ inch from each measurement, make matching measurements and marks in from the edges of a sheet of wallboard, and draw lines connecting the marks. Cut along the shorter line with a keyhole saw (*left*). Score the longer line with a sharp utility knife, prop the sheet behind the scored line with two long 2-by-4s and push down the edge of the sheet abruptly to snap the core (*right*). Slice through the backing paper between the cut pieces and install the sheet.

Fitting around pipes and ducts. If a pipe runs through the wall, toenail a horizontal 2-by-4 below the pipe to the stud on each side, fasten the pipe to the 2-by-4 with a metal pipe strap and nail a vertical 2-by-4 next to the pipe between the horizontal 2-by-4 and the top plate of the wall (inset, left). For a duct, toenail horizontal 2-by-4s ¾ inch above and below the duct and nail vertical 2-by-4s ¾ inch to each side (inset, right).

Measure from the ceiling to the top and bottom of the pipe or duct and to the centers of the horizontal 2-by-4s; measure from the nearest sheet of wallboard to the left and right edges of the pipe or duct and to the center of the vertical 2-by-4s. Transfer all these measurements to a sheet of wallboard, then outline the pipe or duct and the 2-by-4s. Cut a hole for the pipe or duct with a keyhole saw and cut the wallboard along the centers of the 2-by-4s, so it will fit around the pipe like a jigsaw puzzle. Nail the larger piece to the wall, then the smaller one.

Extra Safety from a Sprinkler System

A home sprinkler system, a less extensive version of the ones that protect factories, warehouses and office buildings, does more than retard fires; it puts them out. Installing a sprinkler system throughout an existing house is prohibitively expensive, but adding one to a basement *(below)*—where serious fires often start—is a straightforward job for any skilled amateur plumber.

Sprinklers are excellent protection because they work automatically. Water pipes, fed by the city water line, run through the ceiling joists of each story of the house. Sprinkler heads—plain *(inset)* or flush-mounted for concealment—are spaced along the pipes to serve as nozzles. They are turned on by the heat of a fire, each one dousing 200 square feet of floor area.

In a fire, a fusible link in the sprinkler head melts, allowing two struts in the center of the head to fall clear and release a plug. Water pours out, broken into a fine, even spray by a deflector at the bottom of the head.

In the basement installation illustrated, the system and the house water supply are controlled by separate shutoff valves. A backflow check valve keeps sprinkler water out of the domestic water pipes, and a flow sensor sounds an alarm if water moves through the sprinklers. A test valve simulates the discharge of a sprinkler head to test the alarm and measure the flow of water.

If you are building a new home, installation throughout the house is worth considering. The cost is significant—roughly the same as wall-to-wall carpeting for all rooms—but the savings are significant. Most insurance companies offer premium reductions for a professionally installed sprinkler system and some states offer tax advantages.

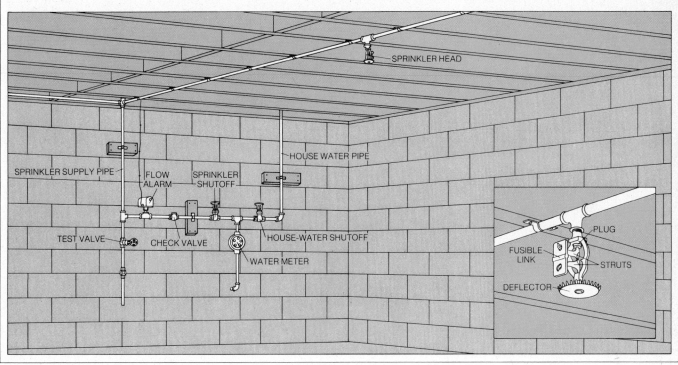

SPRINKLER HEAD

SPRINKLER SUPPLY PIPE — FLOW ALARM — SPRINKLER SHUTOFF — HOUSE WATER PIPE

TEST VALVE — CHECK VALVE — HOUSE-WATER SHUTOFF — WATER METER

PLUG — FUSIBLE LINK — STRUTS — DEFLECTOR

Putting Out a Small Fire with a Hand Extinguisher

Nearly everyone has had an unsettling experience with fire or the threat of fire inside a house. Sometimes the experience—perhaps a frantic search for a cigarette dropped behind a sofa cushion, or a carelessly held potholder smouldering over a stove—is soon ended. Such fires, though potentially dangerous, are generally inconsequential, and easily smothered, brushed away or stamped out.

With a larger fire, such as trash burning in a wastebasket or a pan of grease aflame on the stove, the same measures would be ineffective and dangerous. These fires are serious—yet in their early stages they are often contained in a small space and many can be easily extinguished if you react quickly. Flames in an oven, for example, can be put out by closing the door and turning off the heat. A grease fire in a pan or a deep-fat fryer can be extinguished simply by sliding a metal lid or large baking tin over the pan and turning off the heat. On an electric stove, move the pan to a cold burner.

If you do not have a lid, use salt or baking soda to smother the fire. Sprinkle the fire liberally, but gently to avoid splashing burning grease. Do not use baking powder or flour on flaming grease or carry a pan of burning grease outside.

Never use water to put out either a grease or an electrical fire; it may spread the flames. An electrical fire can often be stopped before it gets well started by pulling the plug or turning off electricity at the service panel. To fight an upholstery fire, on the other hand, water works best. Beat out the flames with a damp towel or douse them with a pan of water. Then carry the cushion or piece of furniture outdoors and soak it thoroughly.

If your clothes catch fire, roll on the ground or floor to smother the flames. Never run. When someone else's clothes are aflame, force the victim to the ground and roll him over and over. Use a rug, blanket or coat to help smother the flames, taking care not to obstruct the victim's breathing. When the fire has been extinguished, keep the victim warm in a clean blanket and call the fire-department rescue service.

All of these small fires, with the single exception of burning clothes, can be put out more safely with portable fire extinguishers, which allow you to quench the flames from a distance.

Extinguishers come with a variety of fire-fighting agents—a powder of ammonium phosphate, ordinary water or carbon dioxide. Each of these smothers a fire by depriving it of oxygen, and each is specifically designed for one or more types of fire. A Class A fire is fed by a solid fuel, such as wood or paper. A Class B fire involves a burning liquid such as grease. And a Class C fire is one in a live electrical circuit. Use the chart on the opposite page to select fire extinguishers for your home. For complete protection, you will need more than one: an extinguisher used against a class of fire for which it is not clearly labeled can actually increase the intensity of a fire.

Hang fire extinguishers in several locations, and always in the kitchen, garage and basement. Mount the extinguishers near doorways, no more than 5 feet above the floor and as far as possible from spots where a fire is likely to start, such as a stove or a paint-storage area. Learn how to operate each extinguisher you buy, and check extinguishers once a month to see that they are fully charged.

If a fire breaks out, alert others to evacuate the house and to call the fire department. Then if the fire has not spread—and if it is not fed by plastics or foam rubber, which often produce poisonous fumes—use a fire extinguisher to douse the flames by the method shown on the opposite page. If the fire continues to burn after the extinguisher is empty, leave the room, close the door behind you and wait outside for the fire fighters.

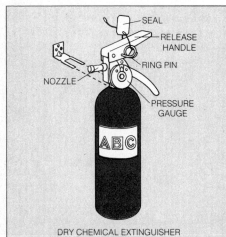

DRY CHEMICAL EXTINGUISHER

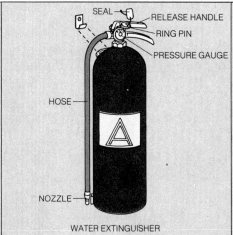

WATER EXTINGUISHER

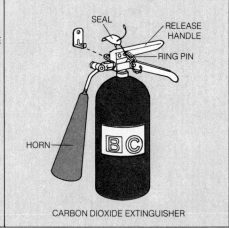

CARBON DIOXIDE EXTINGUISHER

An arsenal of extinguishers. Fire extinguishers of different types can be identified by their appearance as well as by the manufacturer's label. Multipurpose dry chemical models have a stubby nozzle, a water extinguisher has a flexible hose, and a carbon dioxide unit discharges through a horn-shaped nozzle.

Whatever its type, however, each extinguisher hangs from hooks screwed to a wall stud, and has a ring pin or other safety device that immobilizes the release handle to prevent an accidental discharge. A wire or plastic seal, which is easily broken when the ring-pin is removed, shows that the extinguisher has not been used.

The Right Type for Every Blaze

Type of extinguisher	Class of fire	Capacity	Weight	Range of stream	Discharge time	Advantages	Limitations
Multipurpose (Dry chemical)	A, B or C	5 lbs. 10 lbs. 20 lbs.	10 lbs. 21 lbs. 36 lbs.	5-12 ft. 5-20 ft. 5-20 ft.	8-10 sec. 10-25 sec. 10-25 sec.	Puts out all classes of fires; light-weight; inexpensive	May not completely extin-guish a deep-seated upholstery fire; leaves residue
Stored pressure Water	A	2½ gal.	30 lbs.	30-40 ft.	1 min.	Longer discharge time; greater range	Must be protected from freezing; initial dis-charge might create more smoke, making visibility difficult
Carbon dioxide	B or C	5 lbs. 10 lbs. 20 lbs.	16-20 lbs. 33-38 lbs. 52-59 lbs.	3-8 ft. 3-8 ft. 3-8 ft.	8-30 sec. 8-30 sec. 10-30 sec.	Leaves no residue	Dissipates in wind; carbon dioxide "snow" may burn skin; eliminates oxygen around immediate area

Selecting an extinguisher. The main purpose of this chart is to help you balance the advantages and limitations of various fire extinguishers. Multipurpose dry chemical models, for example, which are intended for all kinds of fires, make it unnecessary to classify a fire before extinguishing it. Though lighter and less expensive than other kinds, they leave behind a powder that is difficult to clean up and that does not work as well against Class A fires as water. A water extinguisher, though limited in application, lets you fight a fire longer and at a safer distance than other types. Carbon dioxide extinguishers, more costly than dry chemical or water models, leave no residue after a Class B or C fire. Whichever you choose, buy extinguishers approved by Underwriters' Laboratories and at least the size of the smallest units in the chart. Larger units expel their contents at a faster rate to put out a fire quicker, but they are heavy and offer little improvement in range or discharge time.

How to Use an Extinguisher

Operating a fire extinguisher. Pull the ring pin from the extinguisher to free the release handle, stand at least 5 feet from the fire and discharge the extinguisher at the base of the flames by squeezing the release handle. If the extinguisher stream splatters burning material, back away from the fire, then play the stream on the fire, sweeping slowly from side to side, until you have emptied the extinguisher.

Ladders to Help You Get out of a Burning House—Fast

When flames leap from a basement, or a smoke alarm *(pages 73 and 90)* clamors in the night, there is time for one thing only: escape. A quick exit from a burning house depends partly on early warning, partly on a workable escape plan.

Ideally, every room should have two possible exits, a door and a window. Each family member should know how to leave quickly by every exit and how to do so safely. Family fire drills may be necessary to practice climbing through windows, especially windows that are small and relatively inaccessible, such as those in a basement. Each drill should end at a predetermined meeting spot outside the house so that in a real fire you can tell quickly whether anyone is trapped inside. Post your plan, with exits and the meeting spot clearly marked, on a floor plan of the house, where guests and baby-sitters can see it.

For a one-story house such an escape plan, spelled out in detail and practiced, is generally adequate. But in a two- or three-story house a ladder may be needed to make a fire exit of an upper-floor window, unless it opens onto a porch or garage roof. The ladder may be flexible or rigid, portable or permanently mounted.

A rigid ladder, permanently fastened to the side of the house, is generally preferable (although it may make upper floors accessible to intruders). Most have to be custom-made to match the structure of the house so that they can be attached securely to studs and joists, which can vary in spacing. Usually the professional who makes the ladder also installs it.

Flexible ladders are easily installed. They are inexpensive and inconspicuous but somewhat difficult for any but the agile and cool-headed to use in an emergency. Such a ladder should be made of chain or steel cable and fitted with spacers or "standoffs" to keep the rungs away from the wall for toe- and handholds. One type of flexible ladder requires no installation. It is kept in a box out of the way, then quickly taken out and hung from the window frame when needed *(below)*. Other types are anchored permanently near the window. The widely used model opposite, fitted by the purchaser with standoff rungs for the stool and exterior sill, is always ready in its box at the window if a fire strikes.

Cable-tied Rungs Ready to Hang from a Sill

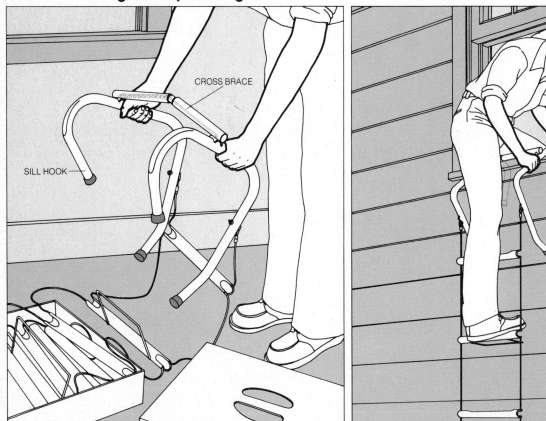

CROSS BRACE

SILL HOOK

1 **Assembling the ladder.** Remove the lid of the ladder box, grasp a sill hook in each hand and pull the hooks out of the box; a spring-and-rod assembly inside a cross brace automatically snaps the hooks together to make a rigid frame.

2 **Using the ladder.** Drop the rungs out of the window and hook the frame over the sill. Climb sideways out the window, straddling the sill so that you can see the ladder beneath you and place your foot on a convenient rung.

What to Do if Fire Breaks Out

Leave the house immediately. Do not stop to dress or to collect valuables. On the way out, close doors to retard the progress of fire and smoke.

Avoid smoke if you can. If you cannot, crawl on hands and knees. You will be below most of the smoke and carbon monoxide, and above dense toxic gases that settle near the floor.

If safety is beyond a closed door, feel the door before you open it. If the surface is cool, open the door slightly to check for heat, flames or smoke before going through it. If the surface feels hot, do not open the door—use an alternate escape route.

If you must open a window to escape, first close all doors to the room. An open door can cause a draft that may draw smoke and flames into the room. If you must break the window, stand back and throw a hard object through it. Take time to clear glass fragments from the frame to prevent cuts as you climb through it.

If you are trapped above the ground floor, do not jump until it is absolutely necessary. To postpone jumping as long as possible, close the door to the room and stuff cloth under it to keep out smoke. Open the window several inches and breathe through the opening. When fire fighters arrive, wave your arms or brightly colored fabric to attract their attention.

If you must jump to safety from the second story or above, climb out the window feet first with your stomach on the sill. Lower yourself as far as possible, then drop, bending your knees when you hit the ground to cushion your fall. If there are children with you, drop them to the ground or to a waiting adult before you jump.

2 **Attaching the handhold rung.** Before installing the top two rungs—the rest of the ladder comes preassembled—lower the ladder from the window. Then place the handhold rung between two chain links that lie opposite each other on the window stool, pass a rung bolt through one of the small spacers, one of the links at the stool, and the handhold rung. Finally, push the bolt through the opposite link on the other chain and through the other small spacer, then attach the nut (inset).

A Permanent Escape Ladder Anchored to the Floor

1 **Fastening the ladder to the floor.** Slip the end link of each chain through the slot in the center of a floor plate. Secure the links, using the curved metal pins that are provided by the manufacturer.

Place the ladder box centered under the escape window, bore pilot holes for the lag screws provided, drilling through the holes in the bottom of the box, and screw the floor plates and box together to the floor.

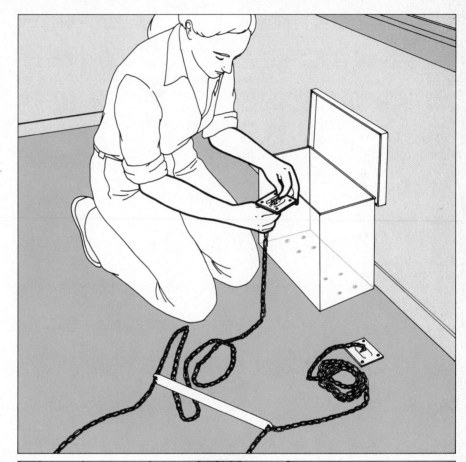

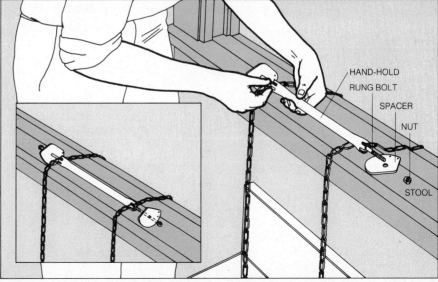

HAND-HOLD
RUNG BOLT
SPACER
NUT
STOOL

3 **Fastening the spacer to the chain.** Before
tightening the assembly, rotate the spacer so that
the round portion rests on the stool and be
sure that the chain links fit into the slots at each
end of the rung. Fasten the chain to each
spacer with the U bolts supplied with the ladder.

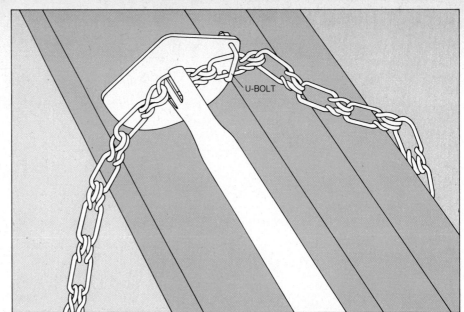

4 **Attaching the standoff rung.** Hold a standoff
spacer alongside one of the chains so that the
center of the spacer's curved portion rests against
the edge of the sill and mark with tape the link
that lines up with the bolthole in the spacer. Repeat for the other chain. Assemble the standoff rung and spacers *(page 111, Step 2)* and fasten
the chains to the standoff spacers with U bolts
(Step 3, above). The ladder can now be pulled up
and stored in its box, ready for use.

How the Pros Fight a Fire

The first rule of fire fighting—rescue the occupants—has not changed since the picturesque days of leather helmets and steam pumpers *(below)*. But the other rules have been altered radically by modern research. Today fire fighters attack household conflagrations with the practiced skill of a well-drilled military unit assaulting an enemy position.

Unlike a homeowner who douses a blaze in a wastebasket, the professionals do not try to extinguish extensive flames immediately. Rather, fire fighters initially protect "exposures"—nearby rooms or buildings—and confine the flames to a restricted area. Only then do they go after the "seat" of the fire.

Fire-fighting techniques have also been modified by research. Studies have shown that fire generally is carried by superheated gases, rather than by the flames themselves. As gases with temperatures in excess of 1,400° F. roll through the house, whole rooms become so hot that they spontaneously explode in flame—a phenomenon firemen call "flashover."

To prevent flashover—and to remove heat and smoke so that fire fighters can get close enough to attack the fire directly—a principal weapon is not water but ventilation, which gets the superheated gases out of the building. Thus the professionals' method is opposite to the one recommended for an amateur: instead of closing windows to block drafts, they break windowpanes so that cool air from outside can replace incendiary gases within.

Simultaneously with ventilation goes the use of water—sometimes mixed with chemicals—to confine and extinguish the blaze. Today, the water is seldom applied as a heavy stream, because water can cause as much property damage as the fire. Modern fire-hose nozzles can be adjusted to throw out a mistlike spray as well. Fire fighters generally fill an entire burning room with the spray, so that a thick cloud of water vapor smothers the blaze. The result, paradoxically, is a completely dry room, in which every drop of water has been used up putting out the fire.

Fire fighting the old way. An insurance advertisement from the 1890s glorifies the heroic, but often misdirected, efforts of old-time fire fighters.

4

Coping with Everyday Hazards

An easy fix for a wobbly rail. Metal braces meant to repair loose chair legs can be screwed to floor and newel post to steady a hazardously shaky handrail. A less visible but more complex solution to this common problem is to secure the newel post with a lag bolt *(page 123)*.

Home is second only to the automobile as a dangerous place to be: household accidents kill 24,000 Americans and injure 3,500,000 each year. Fire, surprisingly, is by no means the principal danger that lurks in a house. About 80 per cent of home mishaps are caused by mundane hazards like slippery bathtubs and poisonous cleaners, medicines and other compounds kept around the house. Many of the victims are visitors to a house who are unaware of hazards that the occupants have learned to avoid.

Some accidents are genuinely unavoidable—an elderly person who loses his balance on stairs, for example, is likely to be injured despite every effort to make the stairway safe. But you can avert many other accidents by noticing and correcting obvious hazards. Look for accidents waiting to happen. Discard or repair pots and pans, for example, with broken or insecure handles. Make sure that sturdy step stools and ladders are handy where they may be needed. Store poisons separately from medicines; segregate over-the-counter medications from prescriptions and separate medicines taken internally from those applied externally. For anyone living in the house who has poor vision, label medicine bottles, and the "on" and "off" positions of kitchen-range knobs, with large letters or with glued-on tactile markers—pieces of sandpaper are easy to feel.

Falls hurt more people in their homes than any other single kind of accident; Americans tumble down the equivalent of a 3,500-mile stairway every year. Pages 120-127 tell you how to make this type of accident less likely by mounting grab bars and applying nonslip grip strips to bathtubs and showers, installing an additional handrail to stairways and strengthening existing banisters that have become rickety *(opposite)*. Carpeting or nonskid wax can add a margin of safety by improving traction on floors and stairways—and carpeting also will cushion the blow if a fall should occur. If a member of your family is infirm or handicapped, there are other special modifications that you can make to your house, such as a gently sloping ramp to an entranceway, extra handles for closing doors and special alterations to bathrooms and closets *(pages 130-133)*.

Locks and fences, which in one form protect your home from intruders as described in Chapter 1, also work to protect you and others from a variety of dangers in and around your home. A gate at the top of a flight of stairs keeps an infant safe from falling down the stairs. Fences outdoors keep toddlers from wandering off or deter neighborhood children who might sneak into a swimming pool *(pages 116-119)*. And lightweight locks, though they may be too flimsy to thwart a burglar, keep poisons, strong medicines, firearms and other household dangers safely out of the hands of youngsters.

Easy-to-Build Garden Fences to Make a Yard Safe

For many homeowners it is the threat of accidents rather than intruders that calls for the building of fences. In some areas, in fact, safety fences are required by building codes; a typical requirement, designed to keep toddlers from tumbling into a swimming pool, specifies a fence at least 6 feet high, with a gate latch 4 feet off the ground.

A chain link fence *(pages 8-13)* will meet this and other safety requirements around a home, but such a fence is not always best. You may want an enclosure that can be quickly put up and dismantled, such as a dog run; or your community may prohibit metal fencing.

Several alternatives are available. Local codes may permit the simplest safety fence of all—a wire-mesh barrier *(below)*, comparable to a chain link fence, but without a top rail for lateral support or tension devices to keep the mesh taut;

the installer simply drives fence posts into the ground, stretches the mesh over prongs on each post and puts in a gate. Wire mesh can also be wrapped around a deck to prevent children from falling between widely spaced railings; or it can be strung along a wrought-iron fence.

Wooden fences of the post-and-rail or stockade types *(pages 117-119)* are equally versatile. Both can be mounted on a wooden retaining wall or a deck by simply bolting the fence posts to the wall timbers or deck joists. Of the two types, the stockade fence is easier to put up, since it does not require dadoes, or grooves, as does a post-and-rail fence. Plan these fences as you would a chain link fence *(page 8)*, but with some variations in post spacing. The round posts for a stockade fence must be located on 8-foot centers so that the facing material, which comes in sections of that length,

can be nailed to them. For a post-and-rail fence *(Steps 1 through 6)* you can locate the posts at any equal intervals up to 8 feet; on a wire-mesh fence, the spacing can be as much as 10 feet.

Wire mesh with a vinyl coating—attractive and rust-resistant—is often preferred. For wooden fences, buy pressure-treated lumber, which resists rot and fungus, or coat the wood with a commercial preservative; use hot-dipped galvanized nails to prevent rust stains. Wooden posts are generally sunk 32 inches into the earth, and must be ordered 32 inches longer than their height aboveground. If you want a post-and-rail fence with a level top, like the one shown on these pages, increase the length of the posts to compensate for the slope of the terrain. Finally, specify gateposts slightly larger than line posts—4-by-6s or 4-by-8s, for example, if the line posts are 4-by-4s.

A Low Wall of Wire Mesh

A wire-mesh enclosure. Rust-resistant metal posts, horseshoe-shaped in cross section and fitted with integral anchor plates, support this wire-mesh fence at 10-foot intervals; the lightweight wire mesh, stretched taut by hand, is hooked to metal prongs on the posts. Corner posts are stood at a 45° angle so that the wire can be stretched easily around the curved rib *(inset)*. A chain link gate secured to the posts with tie wire completes the installation.

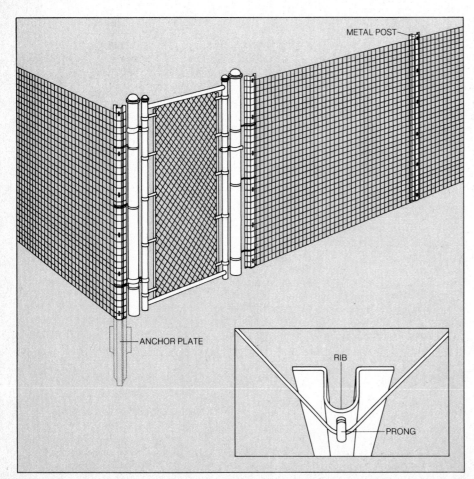

METAL POST

ANCHOR PLATE

RIB

PRONG

Putting Up a
Post-and-Rail Fence

1 **Bracing the first post.** Mark the locations of the posts and gate with stakes *(page 9, Step 1)*. At the highest point along the fence line, dig a hole three times as wide as the post and 36 inches deep. Pour 4 inches of gravel into the hole, set the post in place and drive two stakes on adjacent sides of the hole; fasten 1-by-2 braces to the post and, as a helper plumbs the post, nail the braces to the stakes. Overfill the hole with a thick mixture of ready-mix concrete, tamp the concrete down into the hole and trowel the excess concrete downward from the post to provide for water runoff.

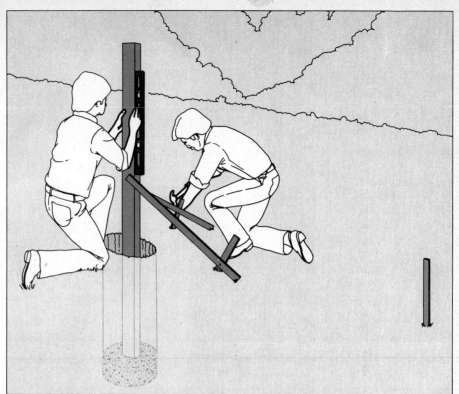

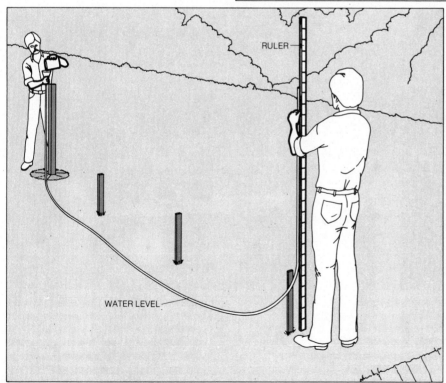

2 **Leveling the posts.** Run a water level from the top of the first post to the lowest point along the fence line. Have a helper hold a folding ruler upright at the low stake, fill the water level even with the top of the post, and have your helper read the height of the water at the stake. Cut a second post to this height plus 32 inches, anchor it *(Step 1)* and stretch a line between the tops of the two posts. At intermediate stakes, measure down from the line to determine the heights of the other posts. If the terrain slopes more than 2 inches per foot, place the water level at a lower point on the first post to maintain a more uniform fence height.

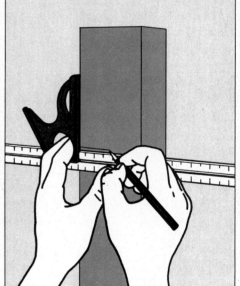

3 **Marking dadoes for the rails.** Using a combination square, make a mark 6 inches below the top of each post and extend it across all sides of the post. Add a mark 1½ inches above the line on the left side of the post, and another 1½ inches below the line on the right side. Extend the marks across both sides of the post. For the bottom rails, make a mark 6 inches up from the ground and use a water level to mark each adjacent post at the same height.

On the corner posts, position the dadoes so that they are at right angles to each other.

4 Cutting the dadoes. Run a circular saw set to a depth of 1½ inches along the lines you made in Step 3, then cut out the dadoes with a mallet and a chisel. Caution: if you are unable to get a firm foothold, use a backsaw instead of a circular saw to make the cuts.

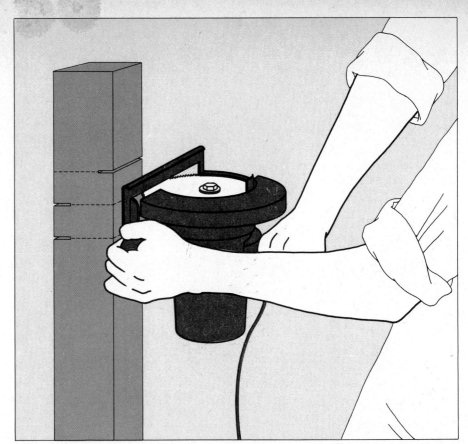

5 Seating the rails. Cut 2-by-4 rails equal to the distance between adjacent posts plus 3 inches and insert the rails into the dadoes. Toenail the rails to the posts. To avoid splitting the wood, blunt the tips of the nails.

6 **Installing the facing.** Cut a 1-by-6 or 1-by-8 2 inches shorter than the height of the fence at a corner. Set it flush with the top and outer edge of the corner post and nail it to the post and both rails. Allowing for the same 2-inch clearance from the ground, cut the remaining boards to size, set them flush with each other along the length of the post and nail them in place. Finally, nail metal caps (*inset*) onto the posts.

For prefabricated stockade fencing, center the ends of each 8-foot section on adjacent posts and nail the section to the posts.

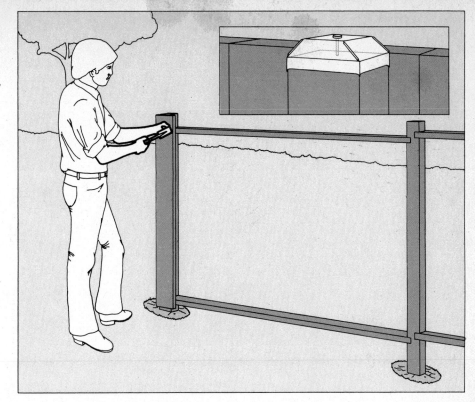

A Gate for a Wooden Fence

Building and hanging the gate. Cut fence boards (*Step 6, above*) and two 1-by-8 braces to the width of the gate. Lay the boards on a flat surface and screw the braces to them, 6 inches from the top and bottom. Cut the ends of a third brace to fit diagonally between the first two, and screw it to the gate.

Set the gate on scraps of wood to center it in the fence opening, flush with the back of the gate-post. Mark the post at the top and bottom of each horizontal brace, remove the gate and attach a hinge centered on each pair of marks. Then reposition the gate, mark the hinge locations on the braces and bolt the flange of each hinge to a brace.

Nail a 1-by-1½-inch wood strip, set flush with the front of the latch post, to serve as a gatestop, and install a latch bar on the gate and a latch on the post. For the string latch pictured here, drill a hole through the latch post and attach the string to the latch (*inset*).

Defusing the Dangers of Bathrooms and Stairs

Accidental injuries occur more often in the home than anywhere else. Most household accidents are of the roller-skate-on-the-stairs variety—avoidable by using common sense. Others may be caused by the design of a house—the fashionable "dropped living room," one step down from the main floor, leads to countless wrenched ankles.

Still other accidents occur despite good design and common caution—bathrooms and stairways, which are responsible for most injuries in the home, are dangerous even if they are built correctly and used with care. But there are things you can do to make these two parts of the house safer.

Stairways are discussed in detail on pages 122-127. In bathrooms, the major cause of accidents is a slippery tub or shower stall. Textured grip strips, usually sold in precut lengths, can be stuck to the bottom of a tub or to the floor of a shower stall to help reduce this danger. (For potentially slippery areas in other rooms—in front of a sink or a washing machine, for example—there is a heavy-duty tape, usually sold in rolls, coated with carborundum, a tough abrasive.)

The durability of such tape depends largely on the smoothness and cleanness of the surface beneath. Wash the surface thoroughly, scraping off any old or curled strips with a putty knife and a solvent such as alcohol or lacquer thinner. Then lay out a pattern for the strips and stick them in place as shown below and at the top of the opposite page.

Even with grip strips, however, you can slip and fall. To lessen that risk, install grab bars (opposite) to provide handholds. You can buy special grab bars or use sturdy towel bars. Either should be at least 18 inches long, free of sharp corners and made of metal tubing.

Creating a Slip-Resistant Surface

Patterns for grip strips. In a shower (right, top) lay grip strips in a star pattern radiating from the center of the shower floor. Use six full-length strips for the long rays and three strips cut in half for the short rays. Round corners so they will not curl. In a bathtub (right, bottom) center a wedge of four full-length strips around the drain, then add three additional strips at the other end of the tub, parallel to the sides.

For a nonslip surface in front of a utility sink or a washing machine cut 20-inch lengths of 1-inch-wide carborundum tape and round the corners. Arrange the strips at 3-inch intervals parallel to the front edge of the sink or washer.

Installing grip strips. Peel away an inch of the paper backing and stick the end of the strip to the surface. Slowly peel off the backing and press the strip against the surface. Finally, press the strip with a wallpaper-seam roller.

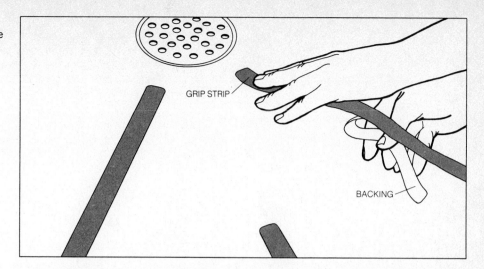

GRIP STRIP

BACKING

Grab Bars for Shower and Bath

1 Positioning grab bars. On the wall of a shower stall or next to a tub, center a grab bar 45 inches above the bottom. If you must drill through tile, rubber-cement an index card to the wall behind each flange and mark fastener holes on the cards. For a tub, add a lower bar 33 inches above the tub bottom. Drill $^3/_{32}$-inch test holes through the cards, using a masonry bit for tile. Apply light pressure and drill at low speed to avoid breaking the tile, then peel the file cards from the wall.

Wherever the wall is hollow, enlarge the test hole to ½ inch for toggle bolts. Wherever the scout bit strikes a stud, drill pilot and shank holes for a No. 8 wood screw 2 inches long.

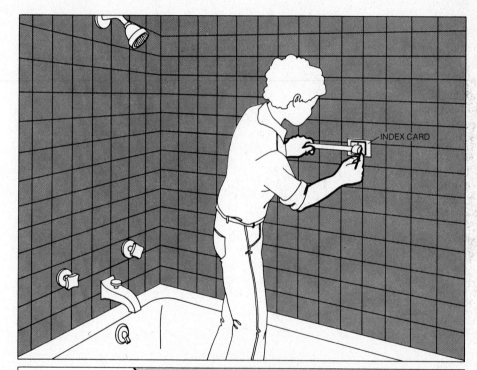

INDEX CARD

2 Fastening a grab bar. Insert $^3/_{16}$-inch toggle bolts 3 inches long through flange holes where the wall is hollow. Fill the inside of each flange with silicone caulk, then start all the toggles into the wall before pushing any of them all the way in. Tighten the bolts. Then, wherever there is a stud behind the flange, drive a wood screw. Finally, caulk around each grab-bar flange.

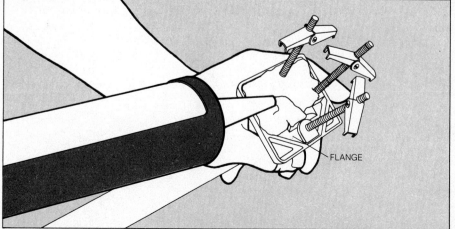

FLANGE

For Stairways, Firm Handholds

Stairways are the most dangerous part of a house, surpassing even bathrooms as a site of accidents. Some stairs have trouble built into them. They can be too steep. Tall or uneven risers invite climbers to trip on tread nosings. Shallow treads make stairs difficult to descend without catching a heel on a riser or slipping over a nosing. Stairways with these deficiencies cannot be made safe; the stairs should be replaced. Other unsafe stairways have no risers at all, but the danger of catching a foot between treads can be eliminated by nailing risers to the boards that support the treads.

Even a well-designed staircase is no guarantee against accidents. The steps may be treacherously slick; the newel posts, which anchor the balustrades, may have loosened with age. And very few staircases are built with a handrail on the stairway wall, a basic safeguard against a disastrous fall. All of these hazards should be corrected by the methods described below.

The slipperiest stairs are those with a natural finish. If you insist on the beauty of bare wood, use nonskid wax on your stairs. It is safer to cover them up with something less slippery. If you choose carpeting, use a low-pile variety—it is less likely to catch a heel or to make a tread seem wider than it is—but unless you are confident of your carpeting skills, have the job done professionally. Carpeting that is poorly installed is more hazardous than no carpeting at all. On basement or attic stairs, where the luxury of carpet may be inappropriate, tack rubber safety treads to the wooden ones, apply heavy-duty grip strips *(pages 120-121)* to treads or coat the treads with paint that contains pumice.

The method for securing a loose newel post depends on the kind of stairway you have. If the bottom step is a bullnose tread *(opposite, top)*, secure the newel with a lag bolt screwed into the post from below. If there is no bullnose, try to examine the underside of the stairway. If you see a 2-inch board at the side or center of the staircase, cut out to support the treads, you have a carriage-mounted stairway (the cutout board is technically called a carriage). Bolt the newel to the outside carriage *(opposite, center)*.

If the underside of the stairs is covered, slip the blade of a knife under the board at the wall end of the treads. If the knife slides well below the board, use the newel-to-carriage method of securing the newel post. If it strikes wood at a depth of about ½ inch, there are no carriages in the staircase: you must tighten the newel by replacing its screws with new ones a size larger or, if the screws are inaccessible, with 1-inch chair-leg braces *(opposite, bottom)*. If the knife test seems inconclusive, break a peephole through the wall under the stairs to find out what type of stairs you have.

If your stairway is less than 36 inches in width, a second handrail is not advisable—it would make the stairway dangerously narrow. Otherwise, you can mount a sturdy handrail on the wall beside the stairs, using metal brackets screwed to the wall studs *(pages 124-127)*. You will need a length of hardwood handrail stock a few inches longer than the distance between the nosing of the bottom tread and the landing at the top of the stairs.

Of the various handrail styles available, order one that measures no more than 2¼ inches at its widest; wider rails are difficult to grasp. At the same time, buy two right-angle handrail sections, called level quarter-turns, that match the stock you select, and two wooden end plates called rosettes. Quarter-turns and rosettes join the handrail to the wall so that someone using it can tell without looking that he is near the top or bottom step.

With a second handrail in place, the stairs are as safe as possible for everyone except crawling or toddling children. To keep them from tumbling down the stairs, close off the top of the staircase with an expanding gate *(page 127)*.

Securing a Loose Newel

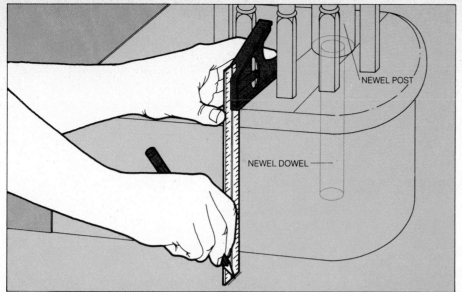

Reinforcing a post in a bullnose. Draw parallel lines across the tread touching the bottom of the newel and, using a combination square, mark the floor below the ends of the lines. Center a nail between each pair of marks and drive it through the flooring. Measure from one nailhead to the newel post and add one half the newel-post diameter. Working underneath the floor, from the basement or the story below, use this measurement and the nail points to find the center of the newel dowel. Drill pilot and shank holes (*page 21*) for a $5/16$-inch lag bolt 3 inches long, then screw the bolt through the flooring into the end of the post.

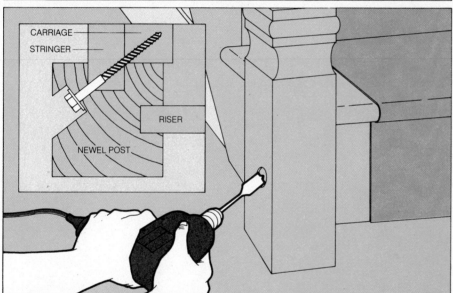

Bolting a newel to a carriage. At the center of the newel post, 4 inches above the floor, use a ¾-inch spade bit to drill a countersink hole ¾ inch deep toward the carriage (*inset*), then bore pilot and shank holes (*page 21*) into the carriage for a $5/16$-inch lag bolt 4 inches long. Fit a washer onto the lag bolt and drive the bolt into the carriage with a socket wrench. Plug the countersink hole with a dowel.

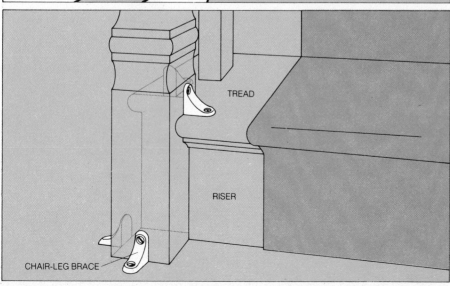

Bracing a newel post. Push the newel post from side to side and spread woodworking glue in any cracks that open between the post and the floor or bottom step. Then fasten chair-leg braces at different heights against opposite sides of the newel post—all four sides, if possible—and to the floor, riser or tread. Attach one brace at a time. Have a helper hold the newel in place while you position a 1-inch brace in a corner and mark for screw holes. Drill pilot holes angled slightly away from the joint for the shankless wood screws that come with braces.

Adding a Rail to a Stairway Wall

1 **Positioning brackets.** Measure the vertical distance from the nosing of the bottom tread to the underside of the existing handrail. Transfer the measurement, less the height of a handrail bracket, to the stairway wall above the bottom-tread nosing and above the upper-landing nosing. With a helper, snap a chalk line between the marks. Using test holes drilled along the chalk line and above nails that fasten the stairway stringer to studs, find the studs at the top and bottom of the stairs; then find every second stud between them and mark the stud widths on the wall.

NOSING

NOSING

STRINGER

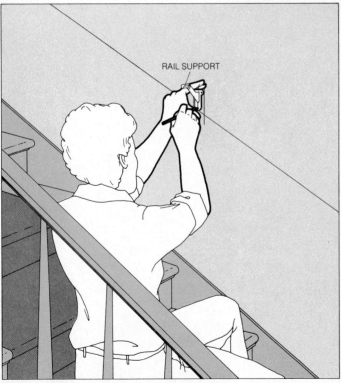

RAIL SUPPORT

2 **Securing brackets to the wall.** Center a hand-rail bracket over each stud, bottom edge at the chalk line, and mark screw holes on the wall. Drill holes (page 21) for the screws that come with the brackets, and screw each bracket to the wall. Measure and note the distance from the center of the rail support to the wall.

3 **Fitting the handrail.** Lay a length of handrail stock on the stairs against the wall and mark it above the bottom-tread and upper-landing nosings. Cut through the stock at the marks, using a miter box to make square cuts.

4 **Trimming the quarter-turns.** Hold each level quarter-turn in the approximate position it will occupy on the wall and mark it to identify the rail end and the wall end. Subtract the thickness of a rosette from the measurement taken in Step 2. On one leg of a framing square locate the mark that corresponds to this distance and align it with the center of the rail arm. Then draw a line across the wall arm, along the other leg of the square. Cut the wall arm along this line using a miter box, then trim 1 inch from the rail arm.

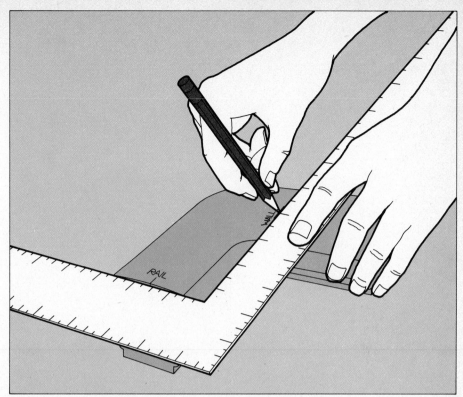

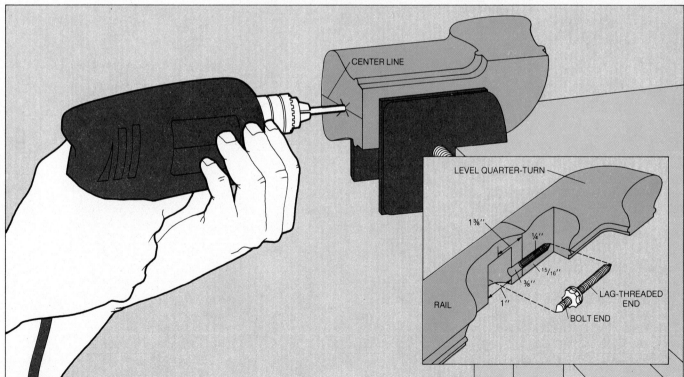

5 **Bolting a quarter-turn to the handrail.** Draw a center line on the rail end of a quarter-turn and mark a point $^{15}/_{16}$ inch above the bottom. Fix the rail arm in a vise and drill a ¼-inch hole, 1⅞ inches deep, in the end. Mark an end of the handrail in the same way; drill a ⅜-inch hole 1⅞ inches deep. Turn the railing over and, 1⅜ inches from the end, drill a 1-inch hole 1½ inches deep. Drill identical holes in the other quarter-turn and in the other end of the handrail.

Run the nut and washer of a rail bolt (*inset*) onto the bolt end of the fastener, then use an adjustable wrench to screw the lag-threaded end into the quarter-turn. Remove the nut and washer and place the bolt end of the fastener into the hole at the end of the rail. Replace the nut and washer through the 1-inch hole in the bottom of the rail and tighten the nut with a nail set. Fill the hole with a wood plug. Fasten the other quarter-turn to the other end of the handrail.

6 **Positioning handrail and rosettes.** With a helper holding the handrail in position on the brackets, set a rosette against the wall at each end of the handrail assembly and trace the outlines of the rosettes on the wall *(right)*.

While your helper pushes the assembly against the wall to hold the rosettes in place, set a handrail clip against the underside of the handrail at each bracket and mark locations for screw holes on the handrail *(inset)*. Remove the assembly and drill pilot holes *(page 21)* for the screws that come with the brackets.

HANDRAIL CLIP

ROSETTE

7 **Securing the rosettes and handrail.** Set each rosette at the outline marked on the wall, drill a $^3/_{32}$-inch hole through the center of the rosette and partway into the wall, then remove the rosette and extend the hole into the wall. If the bit strikes a stud, secure the rosette with a No. 8 flathead wood screw 2½ inches long *(page 21)*; if it does not, use a No. 8S hollow-wall fastener *(page 67)*. Countersink either fastener.

With a helper holding the handrail in position, screw it to each bracket with a handrail clip.

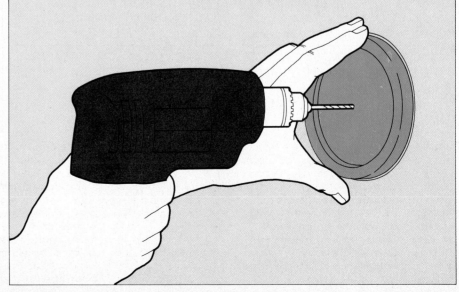

8 **Fastening quarter-turns to rosettes.** Drill 3/32-inch pilot holes and toenail the ends of the handrail assembly to the rosettes, using sixpenny finishing nails. Then countersink the nails and use wood filler to plug the holes.

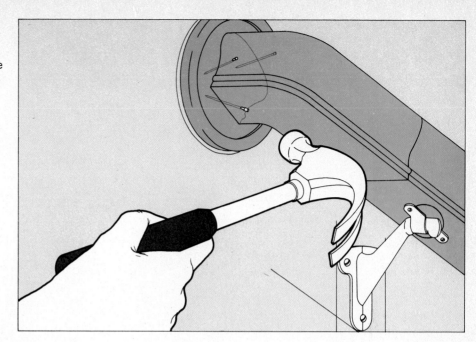

A Safety Gate to Protect Toddlers

END POST

BRACKET

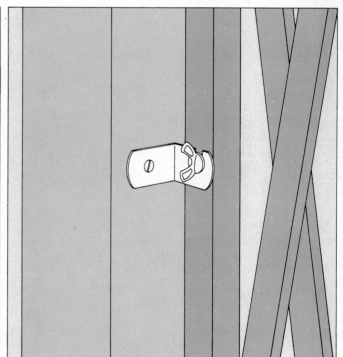

1 **Attaching the gate.** Fit a bracket to the bottom of the end post of the gate and set this post against the wall or newel post, resting the gate on a block to keep it 1½ inches above the landing. Mark a hole on the wall or newel for a bracket fastener and set the gate aside, then attach the bracket with a 2-inch wood screw (*page 21*) or a hollow-wall fastener (*page 67*). Set the gate in the bottom bracket and fit a bracket to the top of the end post. Mark a hole for the upper bracket and attach it with the gate in position.

2 **Installing the catch.** Extend the gate and install its catch according to the manufacturer's instructions; where possible, locate the catch on the stairway side of the gate so a child cannot release it. In the model above, place the catch against the newel post or wall so the slot lies on the stair side of the gate and opens upward. (You may have to reverse the bolt in the gate if the wing nut that secures it lies on the landing side.) Install the catch by one of the methods recommended for the gate brackets (*Step 1*).

Keeping Knives and Poisons out of Reach

In colonial times, a proper housewife wore a ring of keys befitting a jailer, to lock up everything from tea canisters and flatware chests to clothing wardrobes. Those parlous times are gone, but even today the contents of some cabinets and drawers need simple safeguards. In a household with children, you can keep knives, medicines and poisonous products out of reach with a concealed safety latch, screwed inside a wooden cabinet or glued to a metal one; the model at the upper right has an ingenious knob-and-prong fastening that is proof against most youngsters but opens at the touch of an adult's finger.

Elsewhere a cabinet or a chest of drawers may need a true lock to guard its contents. For a cabinet with sliding glass doors, a showcase lock *(lower right)* of the kind used in jewelry stores is adequate, and no lock is easier to install—it simply clamps into place. A cabinet with swinging doors can be fitted with an attractive hasp *(opposite)* that comes with a locking cam rather than a separate padlock. Like a standard hasp-and-padlock assembly, this lock is screwed to the outside of a door.

Installing a recessed drawer lock *(opposite, bottom)* is more involved, and demands some of the intricate joinery used for the dead bolt of a door. Besides a screwdriver, you will need a spade bit to bore a hole for the lock barrel and a wood chisel to cut mortises for the lock plate, lock housing and strike plate.

Childproofing a cabinet. To install this widely available latch, screw or glue the catch no more than 1 inch inside the cabinet top with the prongs projecting inward. Set the ball-tipped end of the latch shaft in the prongs and mark the location of the shaft base on the inside of the door, then fasten the shaft to the door. The shaft will engage the prongs *(inset)* when the door is closed; you release the latch by opening the door just wide enough to slip a finger over the top, then pushing the shaft down and out of the prongs—a trick few young children can master.

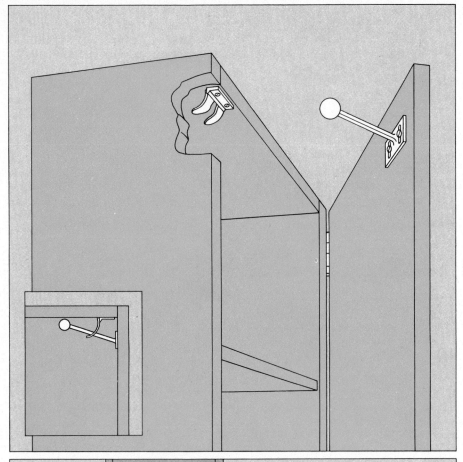

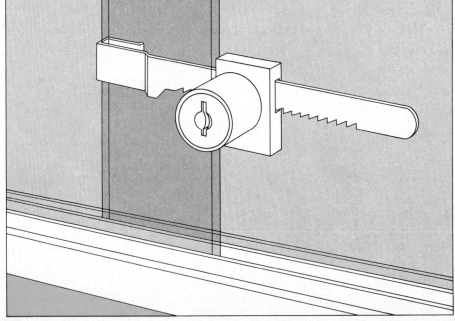

Attaching a showcase lock. With the doors open slip the hook of the lock bar around the edge of the inner door, with the serrated edge of the bar pointing down. Close the doors and slide the lock barrel onto the bar until the barrel is flush with the edge of the outside door. The lock cannot be removed, nor the doors opened, until you unlock the barrel with a key.

Installing a hasp lock. Measure the distance between the centers of the hasp hinge pin and the hasp opening and mark the face of one cabinet door at a point that is one half this distance from the edge of the door. Set the hasp against the door, with its hinge pin centered over the mark; mark the screw holes and attach the hasp to the door. Set the lock against the adjoining door with the cam of the lock protruding through the hasp opening, mark the positions of the lock's screw holes and fasten the lock to the door. You can secure the hasp to the lock by turning the cam 90° with your fingers; to return it to the "open" position, you must use a key.

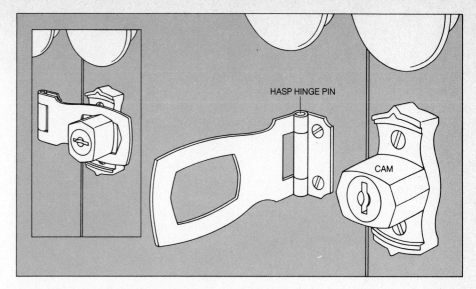

HASP HINGE PIN

CAM

A Recessed Drawer Lock

1 Mounting the lock. To install this lock, you must bore a hole through the drawer front for the barrel; cut a mortise, or recess, in the top of the drawer front for the flange, or lock plate, above the barrel, and cut another mortise in the back of the drawer front for the housing at the base of the barrel (the drawing at right shows the third part of the job).

Start by measuring the distance from the top of the flange to the center of the barrel (inset), mark this distance down from the top of the drawer and, at the mark, drill a hole through the drawer front for the barrel. Insert the barrel from inside the drawer, mark the length of the flange on the drawer top and cut the flange mortise. Reinsert the barrel, outline the mounting, and cut the mounting mortise. Expand both mortises until the lock fits snugly, then screw the lock in place from inside the drawer.

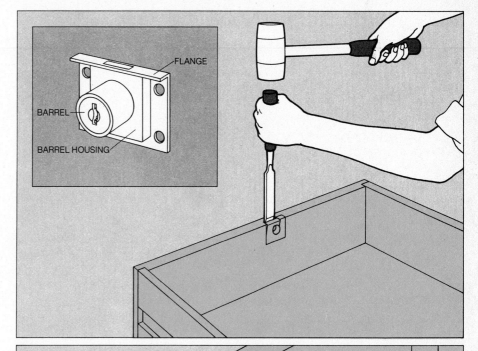

FLANGE

BARREL

BARREL HOUSING

2 Mounting the strike plate. Rub chalk along the top of the bolt, close the drawer fully and use the key to extend the bolt until it presses against the cabinet top. Remove the drawer and, at the chalk mark, cut a hole deep enough to seat the bolt fully (inset); then set the strike plate over the hole, trace its outline and cut a mortise for it. Screw the plate to the cabinet.

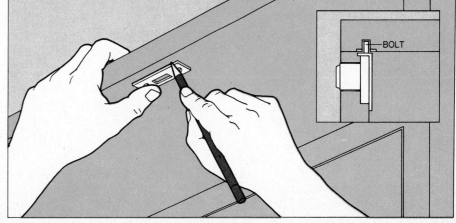

BOLT

Adapting a House to the Needs of the Infirm

Making a home safe and secure for a handicapped or infirm member of the family—without inconveniencing others in the household—can be as simple as reassigning bedrooms, shifting shelves in a closet *(opposite, top)* or rearranging furniture to provide clearance for a walker (27 inches) or a wheelchair (30 inches for passage, 5 feet for turning around). More extensive changes pay big dividends in comfortable living and involve only basic carpentry.

Among the simplest conveniences to add are grab bars. Mounted on doors, they make it easier for a person in a wheelchair to pull the doors closed behind him *(below)*. They are essential in a bathroom; around a tub they must be fastened to walls, but for the toilet there are special models that clamp temporarily to the toilet bowl or bolt to the floor.

Eliminating the biggest obstacle that the handicapped face at home—stairs—requires a ramp to turn the steep rise of steps into a gentle incline. Few houses have room for a ramp indoors, but one to an outside door often can be provided.

The wooden structure shown overleaf has two sections: a sloping ramp and a level landing, both fitted with handrails. These basic components are adaptable to almost any entranceway. You can, for example, use a landing between two ramp sections to make the ramp turn a corner or double back on itself. Such combinations save space in a small yard or make it possible to reach a high doorway. If your house has a porch, you may be able to use the porch as a landing.

The slope of a ramp must not exceed 1 inch of rise for every foot of length. The landing should be 6 feet long—so that a person in a wheelchair can open the door with no fear of rolling backward down the ramp—and offset to give more room on the knob side of the door to make the knob easier to reach. The width of both ramp and landing should be 3½ feet, wide enough for a wheelchair to pass comfortably, yet narrow enough for the person in the chair to pull himself along by grasping the railings.

To build the ramp and landing, you will need 2-by-10s and 2-by-4s for the framing, ¾-inch exterior plywood for decking and 4-by-4 posts set 3 feet into the ground. Use 8-foot posts if the ramp rises no more than 30 inches; above this height, switch to 10-foot posts for the ramp and landing. Buy pressure-treated lumber and plywood to prevent rot, and soak the cut ends of boards with wood preservative before assembling the ramp.

If the route of the ramp is already occupied wholly or in part by a concrete walk, you can let one or two posts rest directly on the concrete; otherwise adjust the width of the ramp or space the posts to make them miss the walk.

A handle and kick plates for a door. Mount a screw-on towel bar 30 inches above the floor on the side of the door that swings into the doorway, so that a person in a wheelchair can use the bar to swing the door shut. On a hollow-core door, attach the handle with machine screws running completely through the door, placing washers under the nuts; on a solid-core door, fasten the bar with 1½-inch wood screws.

Screw metal or plastic kick plates at the bottom of the door to prevent scuffing from wheelchair footrests or walker bars.

Modifying a clothes closet. To place clothes within easy reach from a wheelchair, move the closet pole to a level about 3½ feet above the floor. Install a shelf about 4 feet high and no more than 16 inches deep, so that someone in a wheelchair can reach objects stored at the back of the closet. (Another, higher shelf converts the otherwise useless space above the lower shelf into storage space for an ambulatory person.)

Adapting a bathroom. Install grab bars next to the bathtub and next to the toilet, mounting them on walls by the technique shown on page 121. For fastening a waist-high grab bar to the floor— as you might next to a toilet with no wall nearby—bolt a grab bar to the floor, using the technique described on page 45, Step 2, or page 67. To simplify use of a shower, buy a seat for the tub and install a hand-held shower with a flexible metal hose. To tilt a wall mirror downward slightly so that a person in a wheelchair can see himself, rest the mirror bottom on a strip of wood fitted with mirror clips and fastened to the wall, then tilt the mirror by adjusting the length of the picture wire suspending it.

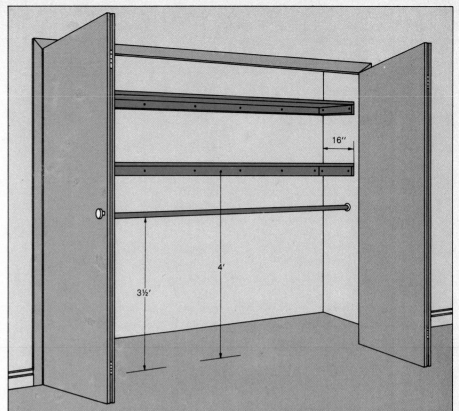

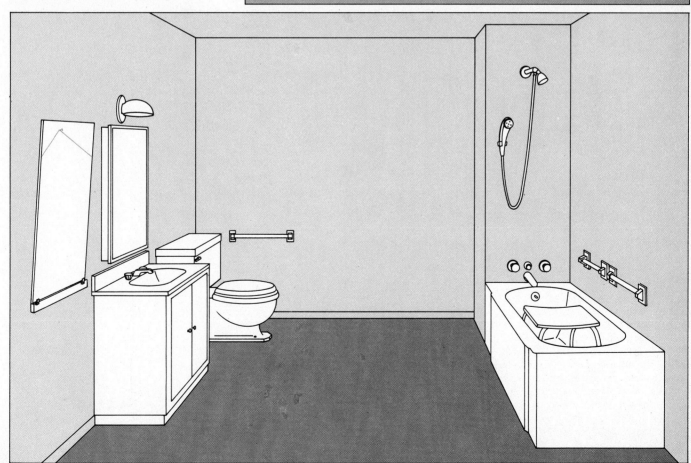

A Ramp to an Entryway

1 Laying out the ramp. Excavate holes 3½ feet deep for 4-by-4 posts along two string lines arranged perpendicular to the house—one line as close as possible to the hinged side of the door, the other 49 inches away on the opposite side of the steps. Dig holes alongside the house-that are wide enough to hold a single post; next dig a pair of holes 6 feet out from the first ones, each big enough for two posts; then space holes for single posts no farther than 8 feet apart along the string lines. If any post positions coincide with the sidewalk, do not dig holes; the posts there can rest on the walk, but you will have to add extra bracing later. Pour 6 inches of concrete into each hole and let it harden. While a helper holds the posts plumb, alternately shovel and tamp earth into the holes, leaving the last foot of the holes at the base of the ramp unfilled.

2 Trenching for the frame. To set the bottom of the ramp at ground level, dig trenches just inside the posts, starting from the bottom end, 10 feet long and 4 inches wide, starting at a depth of 12 inches and sloping upward toward the house 1 inch per foot of length. Dig a trench 7 inches deep between the end posts for the end joist (*inset*). Two feet nearer the house, dig another cross trench to a depth of 5 inches for the second joist up. Pour 2 inches of gravel into the bottoms of the trenches.

3 **Assembling the platforms.** For the ramp, butt-nail 2-by-4 joists 39 inches long between 2-by-10 stringers at the ends and every 2 feet. If necessary, splice stringers with 3-foot lengths of 2-by-10, fastened with at least four nails on each side of the joint. Splices should fall within 2 feet of posts. Cut 36-inch joists to install between splices. If the ramp will straddle a concrete walkway, omit any joist that will not stand clear of the walkway when the ramp is positioned between the posts.

For the landing, cut stringers 6 feet long and join them with joists spaced 2 feet apart.

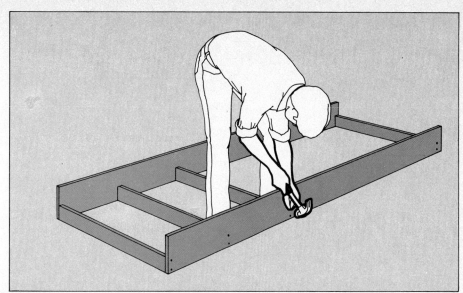

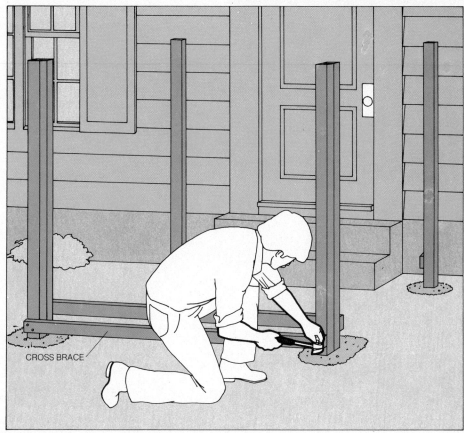

CROSS BRACE

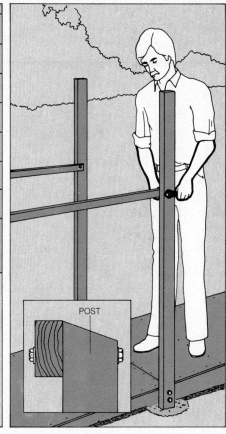

POST

4 **Mounting the undercarriages.** Nail 2-by-4 braces between the posts that will support the landing, placing the braces 10 inches below the level of the door threshold. If steps get in the way of the brace nearest the house, nail 2-by-4 blocks to the insides of the posts instead. Then nail a brace between the posts for the upper end of the ramp, placing it ½ inch below the level of the brace on the adjacent landing posts. Set the landing platform on its braces, then position the ramp platform on its brace at one end and in the trenches at the other. Bolt the stringers to each post with two ⅜-inch galvanized bolts 6 inches long. Use a large washer on each end of the bolts. Cut and install joists to rest on the sidewalk wherever they were omitted in Step 3, but do not fit one at the end of the stringers. Tamp earth around the bottommost posts. Fill the trenches with gravel, then deck the platforms with ¾-inch plywood, making the joints between deck sections fall on the joists.

5 **Installing the handrails.** Fasten 2-by-4 handrails to the posts 30 inches above the deck with ⅜-inch bolts. Trim the posts at the top of the railing but sloped away from it so that the tops of the posts will shed water. Paint the plywood ramp surface with marine deck paint containing pumice, but leave the other wood to weather; painting it could conceal cracks that weaken the structure. Add a grab bar to the door (*page 130*). If you have a screen door, install a grab bar and remove the automatic closer.

Picture Credits

The sources for the illustrations in this book are shown below. The drawings were created by Roger C. Essley, Fred Holz, Judy Lineberger, Peter McGinn and Joan S. McGurren. Credits for the pictures from left to right are separated by semicolons, from top to bottom by dashes.

Cover: Aldo Tutino. 6: Fil Hunter. 8 through 17: John Massey. 18 through 29: Frederic F. Bigio from B-C Graphics. 30 through 37: Walter Hilmers Jr. 38,39: Peter McGinn. 40 through 47: Frederic F. Bigio from B-C Graphics. 49: Guy Gillette, Photo Researchers. 50: Fabbri, Milan. 51: Fabbri, Milan; Robert Perron—Simon Benetton. 52,53: National Trust for Historic Preservation; Fabbri, Milan—Fabbri, Milan; Simon Benetton. 54: Massimo Comandini; National Trust for Historic Preservation. 55: Robert Perron; Eric Russell. 56: Courtesy Airco Welding Products. 58 through 67: Frederic F. Bigio from B-C Graphics. 68: Fil Hunter. 70 through 73: Gerry Gallagher. 74 through 77: Walter Hilmers Jr. 79,80,81: Whitman Studio. 82, 83: Walter Hilmers Jr. 84 through 91: John Massey. 92,93: Eduino Pereira. 94 through 99: Walter Hilmers Jr. 100: Fil Hunter. 104 through 107: Frederic F. Bigio from B-C Graphics. 108,109: Peter McGinn. 110, 111,112: Walter Hilmers Jr. 113: Courtesy Library of Congress. 114: Fil Hunter. 116 through 121: Forte, Inc. 123 through 127: John Massey. 128,129: Peter McGinn. 130 through 133: Whitman Studio.

Acknowledgments

The index/glossary for this book was prepared by Mel Ingber. The editors also wish to thank the following: Bob Adams, Frederick W. Sachs Jr., W. F. Wiseman, W. A. Smoot and Company, Alexandria, Va.; P. Z. Adelstein, Eastman-Kodak Company, Rochester, N.Y.; Al Barsimanto, Midex, Inc., Mountain View, Calif.; John W. Bartley, Arthur Benham and Fred Levering, Baldwin Hardware Manufacturing Corp., Reading, Pa.; Russell Bauer, Master Lock Company, Milwaukee, Wis.; Linda Blanc, National Fire Protection Association, Boston, Mass.; William Borger, Borger Construction, Washington, D.C.; R. Michael Bowman, U.S. Department of Agriculture, Washington, D.C.; Heather Bradley, Liberty Safety and Security Distributers, Baltimore, Md.; James Buck and Nancy Christensen, General Electric Company, Cleveland, Ohio; Waverly Cameron and Fred Campbell, Aritech Company, Framingham, Mass.; Carl Cannella, Dale L. Wentz and J. M. Winge, Sears Roebuck and Company, Chicago, Ill.; Davenport Insulation, Inc., Springfield, Va.; Victor Dixon, Ralph Weatherholtz and Charles Weatherholtz, Lee Fence Company, Fairfax, Va.; Buildex Design, Inc., Alexandria, Va.; David J. Burdick, Tandy Corp., Ft. Worth, Tex.; Copper Development Association, Inc., New York, N.Y.; Tom Crawford, Rohm and Haas, Bristol, Pa.; Herb Curry, General Electric Sheet Products, Pittsfield, Mass.; Vernon Daniel, Manassas, Va.; Decorator Center, Bethesda, Md.; Thomas J. Demont and Robin Lecky, A-1 Lock and Safe Service, Inc., Alexandria, Va.; Lee Dosedlo, Dale McCleary and Ben Zimmer, Underwriters' Laboratories, Northbrook, Ill.; Brian J. Drummond, Westinghouse Electric Corp., Pittsburgh, Pa.; Gerald Duarte, Contra Costa Fire District, Pleasant Hill, Calif.; Gary M. Evans, American District Telegraph, Hyattsville, Md.; Charles O. Everly, Department of Building Inspection, Alexandria, Va.; Gary Fairchild, A-Plus Rental, Springfield, Va.; Aubrey B. Feagans, Alexandria, Va.; Charles Ferst, Versant Corp., Bethesda, Md.; Marion Finney, Scovill, Inc., Cincinnati, Ohio; Bill Fitch, Owens-Corning Fiberglass, Toledo, Ohio; Fox Police Lock Company, New York, N.Y.; Paul Garner, Federal Health Service, Washington, D.C.; Bill Greer, National Burglar and Fire Alarm Association, Washington, D.C.; James M. Haely, The Beltway Fire Equipment Company, Beltsville, Md.; George Hack and Tim Noland, Long Fence, Fairfax, Va.; Martin Hanna, Randallstown, Md.; Hamilton Welding and Iron, Springfield, Va.; Earl Harvey, Gaines Hardware Store, Alexandria, Va.; A. S. Herbert, Second District Police Headquarters, Washington, D.C.; Bruce W. Hisley, Anne Arundel County Fire Department, Millersville, Md.; Robert Hodnett, National Fire Protection Association, Boston, Mass.; Walt Hughes, Diversified Manufacturers, Burlington, N.C.; Peggy Ivey, Creative Concepts, Graham, N.C.; C. N. Jaynes and Crew, Virginia Electric and Power Company, Alexandria, Va.; Nancy Johnston, National Injury Information Clearinghouse, Bethesda, Md.; Don Kaiser, Yale Lock, Charlotte, N.C.; Dick Kessler, Tapeswitch Corporation, Farmingdale, N.Y.; Brent Kington, Southern Illinois University, Carbondale, Ill.; James R. Kogle, Arlington County Police Department, Arlington, Va.; Kragg Kysor, Stanley Hardware, New Britain, Conn.; Kenneth J. Leff, Electro Signal Lab, Inc., Rockland, Mass.; Hap Leibor, Custom Protection Corp. of Alexandria, Alexandria, Va.; Danny Dean Looney, Triangle, Va.; Robert J. Madden, Fire Equipment Manufacturers' Association, Inc., Arlington, Va.; Jim Martin, ABC Fire Protection Service, Falls Church, Va.; Linda McCroddan, Commercial Plastics and Supply, Hyattsville, Md.; Sandy Merrill and Mac Slonecker, Pease Company, Fairfield, Ohio; A. J. Miley, Grinnell Fire Protection Systems Company, Inc., Columbia, Md.; Edward Miller, Safemasters Company, Washington, D.C.; Miller's Hardware, Alexandria, Va.; Charles J. Mirarchi, Scovill, Inc., Springfield, Va.; John Morgan III, Alexandria, Va.; Kathy Murphy, National Center for a Barrier-Free Environment, Reston, Va.; National Association of Fire Equipment and Distributors, Inc., Chicago, Ill.; National Bureau of Standards, Fire Safety Engineering Division, Washington, D.C.; National Safety Council, Chicago, Ill.; The New England Lock and Hardware Company, South Norwalk, Conn.; Michael L. Nicholson and Herman Springs, Alexandria Police Department, Alexandria, Va.; Earl Nuckols Jr., Virginia Safe and Lock Service, Fairfax, Va.; Jim Pendleton, Ray Fox and Robert A. Walker, Good Earth Nursery, Inc., Falls Church, Va.; Paul Ponzelli, Suburban Welding Company, Alexandria, Va.; Nancy Potter, J. L. Fence Manufacturing, Bladensburg, Md.; Mason Powers, Hechinger Company, Alexandria, Va.; John Ragusa, Bel Welding Supply Company, Inc., Hyattsville, Md.; Christopher Ray, Philadelphia, Pa.; Harwood E. Read

III, ADT Security Systems, Landover, Md.; Eric N. Rice-Johnston, Office of the Fire Marshall, Fairfax, Va.; James P. Rosen, The Reinhard Corporation, San Leandro, Calif.; Paul Rummel, Brock Tool Company, Washington, D.C.; Nanette St. Pierre, St. Pierre Manufacturing Corp., Worcester, Mass.; James Scheide and James Stands, Anchor Fence Company, Baltimore, Md.; Steve Schlegel, Pease Company, Springfield, Va.; Allen Setterquist, ITT-Nolub, Sycamore, Ill.; John A. Sharry, National Fire Protection Association, Boston, Mass.; Harry Shaw, National Fire Prevention and Control Administration, Washington, D.C.; Jefferson S. Smith, Custom Construction & Restoration Company, Annandale, Va.; Joseph Sraeel, Airco Welding Products, Inc., Murray Hill, N.J.; Alan Sutherland, Union Hardware Company, Washington, D.C.; Mary E. Sutton, Scotty's Fire Extinguisher Service, Alexandria, Va.; Don Taylor, Fries, Beall and Sharp Company, Springfield, Va.; William B. Taylor, ADT, New York, N.Y.; William L. Testa, Grinnell Fire Protection Systems, Inc., Providence, R.I.; Melvin Waltrous, Fire Marshall's Office, Columbus, Ohio; Mary Ann Waltz, Punch's Pastures Farm, Washington, D.C.; Welding Engineering and Equipment Company, Beltsville, Md.; Buddie White, Bosco Welding Supply Company, Alexandria, Va.; Glenn White, All American Dog Training Academy, Inc., Rockville, Md.

Index/Glossary

Included in this index are definitions of many of the technical terms used in this book. Page references in italics indicate an illustration of the subject mentioned.

Printed in U.S.A.